THE BEDFORD SERIES IN HISTORY AND CULTURE

John Brown's Raid
on Harpers Ferry

A Brief History with Documents

Related Titles in
THE BEDFORD SERIES IN HISTORY AND CULTURE
Advisory Editors: Lynn Hunt, *University of California, Los Angeles*
David W. Blight, *Yale University*
Bonnie G. Smith, *Rutgers University*
Natalie Zemon Davis, *Princeton University*
Ernest R. May, *Harvard University*

Slavery, Freedom, and the Law in the Atlantic World: A Brief History with Documents
Sue Peabody, *Washington State University Vancouver*, and Keila Grinberg, *Universidade Federal do Estado do Rio de Janeiro*

William Lloyd Garrison and the Fight against Slavery: Selections from THE LIBERATOR
Edited with an Introduction by William E. Cain, *Wellesley College*

Women's Rights Emerges within the Antislavery Movement, 1830–1870: A Brief History with Documents
Kathryn Kish Sklar, *Binghamton University, State University of New York*

THE CONFESSIONS OF NAT TURNER *and Related Documents*
Edited with an Introduction by Kenneth S. Greenberg, *Suffolk University*

Defending Slavery: Proslavery Thought in the Old South: A Brief History with Documents
Paul Finkelman, *Albany Law School*

NARRATIVE OF THE LIFE OF FREDERICK DOUGLASS: AN AMERICAN SLAVE, WRITTEN BY HIMSELF *with Related Documents, Second Edition*
Edited with an Introduction by David W. Blight, *Yale University*

The U.S. War with Mexico: A Brief History with Documents
Ernesto Chávez, *University of Texas at El Paso*

DRED SCOTT V. SANDFORD: *A Brief History with Documents*
Paul Finkelman, *Albany Law School*

Abraham Lincoln, Slavery, and the Civil War: Selected Writings and Speeches
Edited by Michael P. Johnson, *Johns Hopkins University*

HOSPITAL SKETCHES *by Louisa May Alcott*
Edited with an Introduction by Alice Fahs, *University of California, Irvine*

UP FROM SLAVERY *by Booker T. Washington with Related Documents*
Edited with an Introduction by W. Fitzhugh Brundage, *University of North Carolina at Chapel Hill*

THE BEDFORD SERIES IN HISTORY AND CULTURE

John Brown's Raid on Harpers Ferry

A Brief History with Documents

Jonathan Earle

University of Kansas

BEDFORD/ST. MARTIN'S   Boston ♦ New York

For Bedford/St. Martin's

Publisher for History: Mary V. Dougherty
Director of Development for History: Jane Knetzger
Developmental Editor: Laurel Damashek
Editorial Assistant: Katherine Flynn
Senior Production Supervisor: Nancy J. Myers
Executive Marketing Manager: Jenna Bookin Barry
Project Management: Books By Design, Inc.
Text Design: Claire Seng-Niemoeller
Index: Books By Design, Inc.
Cover Design: Liz Tardiff
Cover Art: John Brown, 1800–1859, Abolitionist (Detail), Daguerreotype by Augustus Washington (1820/21–?). National Portrait Gallery, Smithsonian Institute/Art Resource, N.Y.
Composition: Stratford/TexTech
Printing and Binding: RR Donnelley & Sons Company

President: Joan E. Feinberg
Editorial Director: Denise B. Wydra
Director of Marketing: Karen Melton Soeltz
Director of Editing, Design, and Production: Marcia Cohen
Manager, Publishing Services: Emily Berleth

Library of Congress Control Number: 2007932895

Copyright © 2008 by Bedford/St. Martin's

Manufactured in the United States of America.

For information, write: Bedford/St. Martin's, 75 Arlington Street, Boston, MA 02116 (617-399-4000)

ISBN-10: 0-312-39280-X
ISBN-13: 978-0-312-39280-2

Foreword

The Bedford Series in History and Culture is designed so that readers can study the past as historians do.

The historian's first task is finding the evidence. Documents, letters, memoirs, interviews, pictures, movies, novels, or poems can provide facts and clues. Then the historian questions and compares the sources. There is more to do than in a courtroom, for hearsay evidence is welcome, and the historian is usually looking for answers beyond act and motive. Different views of an event may be as important as a single verdict. How a story is told may yield as much information as what it says.

Along the way the historian seeks help from other historians and perhaps from specialists in other disciplines. Finally, it is time to write, to decide on an interpretation and how to arrange the evidence for readers.

Each book in this series contains an important historical document or group of documents, each document a witness from the past and open to interpretation in different ways. The documents are combined with some element of historical narrative—an introduction or a biographical essay, for example—that provides students with an analysis of the primary source material and important background information about the world in which it was produced.

Each book in the series focuses on a specific topic within a specific historical period. Each provides a basis for lively thought and discussion about several aspects of the topic and the historian's role. Each is short enough (and inexpensive enough) to be a reasonable one-week assignment in a college course. Whether as classroom or personal reading, each book in the series provides firsthand experience of the challenge—and fun—of discovering, recreating, and interpreting the past.

Lynn Hunt
David W. Blight
Bonnie G. Smith
Natalie Zemon Davis
Ernest R. May

Preface

John Brown's raid on the federal arsenal at Harpers Ferry in 1859 lasted just thirty-six hours, but it was a watershed in American history. No other event during the turbulent decade of the 1850s did more to drive a wedge between the North and the South. In its aftermath, exaggerated reports of Brown's abolitionist network dominated Southern newspapers and rekindled fears of slave insurrection. Southern moderates considered Brown's plot just an opening salvo in a widespread Northern conspiracy to abolish slavery and destroy Southern society. At the same time, many Northerners shocked the South with their sympathy for Brown, especially after he demonstrated an uncanny eloquence at his trial. And the event provided an ever-present backdrop to the pivotal 1860 elections. Whether intentional or not, Brown's raid set North against South so profoundly that the Civil War began less than eighteen months after his execution by the state of Virginia.

This book is the first of its kind to help students understand the historical context, significance, and long-term ramifications of John Brown's raid. It demonstrates how Harpers Ferry became a catalyst for rhetoric and action for both North and South, and for both pro- and antislavery voices. Given the centrality that most U.S. historians place on the Civil War and the conflicting ideologies that precipitated it, learning about Brown's raid and the way it was interpreted should be an essential part of all students' encounters with American history.

The volume's introduction tells the story of how a struggling businessman and father with strong Calvinist beliefs came first to abolitionism, then to action against slavery and in favor of African American rights, and finally to a belief that violence and insurrection were the only means likely to destroy slavery in the United States. More broadly, the introduction emphasizes the many themes that students will find woven throughout the documents:

— The major economic changes sweeping the nation in the nineteenth century
— The expansion of slavery into the West
— The inability of politicians to successfully resolve the slavery issue
— The religious revivals that remade American Christianity
— The rise of movements for social reform, especially abolitionism

The historical documents are presented in four chapters, each providing an exploration of different phases of Brown's evolution from abolitionist to warrior-prophet to martyr. Chapter 1 examines Brown's early abolitionist agitation in New England and his actions in Kansas Territory, where Brown's activities against proslavery settlers brought him national attention. Chapter 2 focuses on the raid on Harpers Ferry and the resulting trial, where Brown coaxed still more notoriety from the ashes of his failed invasion of the South. Chapter 3 illustrates, with Brown's own prison letters, the process by which a condemned man refashioned himself as an abolitionist martyr, and Chapter 4 presents some of the conflicting and momentous responses to Brown's raid in both the North and South.

Each document is introduced with a thoughtful headnote that provides a road map for understanding the sources' contexts and connections; a chronology at the end of the book lays out a timeline of critical turning points in Brown's life and the struggle between pro- and antislavery ideologies in the United States. Additional resources include a detailed dramatis personae of the people involved in the raid and Brown's life; useful maps illustrating the slavery question, "Bleeding Kansas," and the raid at Harpers Ferry; questions for consideration; and a selected bibliography to guide students to further reading.

A NOTE ABOUT THE TEXT

In most circumstances, I have left unchanged the nineteenth-century spelling and punctuation in the documents—the exception being when the meaning itself is obscured. John Brown wrote very deliberately in a mannered style that, at times, mimicked the phrasing and cadences of the writing in the Old Testament. Passages that can at first seem confusing or obscure often, upon further reflection, reveal multitudes about their author and his times.

ACKNOWLEDGMENTS

This book grew out of conversations with Katherine Kurzman and David Blight, and I am indebted to both for their ideas and support. Patricia Rossi and Mary Dougherty gently and kindly prodded the (at times) overcommitted author. Laurel Damashek came aboard this project at a critical time and did a terrific job, and Jane Knetzger, Katherine Flynn, and Nancy Benjamin skillfully guided it to completion. Written comments provided by Amy Greenberg of Pennsylvania State University, Robert Bonner of Michigan State University, Ginette Aley of the University of Southern Indiana, John Sacher of the University of Central Florida, Wade Shaffer of West Texas A&M University, and one anonymous reader made this book infinitely better.

Financial support came from the Henry E. Huntington Library in San Marino, California, and the University of Kansas's General Research Fund. My former colleague and steadfast mentor, Peter Mancall, provided helpful suggestions, and Bradley Freedman and Kristen Epps each worked tirelessly tracking down hard-to-find newspaper editorials and documents. Leslie Tuttle aided the project with her razor-sharp historical eyesight. Karl Gridley, a deep font of Brown knowledge and a wonderful historian, kept me honest. Finally, thanks to the communities of eastern Kansas, especially my hometown of Lawrence, for making it a joy for this scholar to work on Old Osawatomie Brown.

Jonathan Earle

Contents

Foreword   v

Preface   vii

LIST OF MAPS AND ILLUSTRATIONS   xiv

PART ONE
Introduction: Abolitionist, Warrior, Martyr, Prophet   **1**

Brown's Early Life   3
John Brown and the Rise of Abolitionism   5
A Radical Abolitionist   10
Making Kansas Bleed   13
The Plan   19
The Raid   23
The Trial   27
Reckoning with John Brown   32

The Harpers Ferry Raid: Dramatis Personae   **38**

PART TWO
The Documents   **41**

1.   **The Making of a Radical Abolitionist**   **43**

　　1. John Brown, *Words of Advice to the United States
　　　League of Gileadites*, January 15, 1851   43

2. Kansas Territorial Legislature, *An Act to Punish Offenses against Slave Property*, 1855   48

3. John Brown, *Letter to Wife and Children from Kansas Territory*, December 16, 1855   51

4. Mahala Doyle and Louisa Jane Wilkinson, *Accounts of the Pottawatomie Massacre*, 1856   55

5. John Brown, *An Idea of Things in Kansas*, 1857   58

6. John Brown, *John Brown's Parallels: Letter to the Editor of the* New York Tribune, 1859   62

2. The Raid and Trial   **65**

7. John Brown, *Provisional Constitution and Ordinances for the People of the United States*, May 8, 1858   65

8. Osborne Anderson, *A Voice from Harpers Ferry*, 1861   70

9. John Brown, *Interview with Senator James Mason, Representative Clement Vallandigham, and Others*, October 18, 1859   76

10. *Excerpts from the Trial of John Brown*, 1859   85

    Opening Remarks of John Brown to the Virginia Court, October 27, 1859   85

    John Brown's Response to Claims of His Insanity, October 28, 1859   86

    Last Address of John Brown to the Virginia Court, November 2, 1859   86

3. The Making of a Martyr   **88**

11. John Brown, *Selected Prison Letters*, October 21– December 2, 1859   88

4. Responses to John Brown's Raid   **104**

12. *Northern and Southern Newspapers React to the Raid and Trial*, 1859   104

    New Hampshire Patriot, *The Harpers Ferry Affair*, October 26, 1859   105

    Petersburg (Virginia) Express, *The Harpers Ferry Conspiracy*, October 25, 1859   107

Albany, New York, Evening Journal, *From the Philadelphia Press*, November 30, 1859   109

13. Henry David Thoreau, *A Plea for Captain John Brown*, October 30, 1859   110

14. Governor Henry Wise, *Message to the Virginia Legislature*, December 5, 1859   122

15. U.S. Senate Select Committee on the Harpers Ferry Invasion, *The Mason Report*, June 15, 1860   129

16. William W. Patton, *John Brown's Body*, 1862   142

APPENDIXES

A Chronology of John Brown and Events of the Civil War Era (1800–1865)   144

Questions for Consideration   148

Selected Bibliography   150

Index   153

Maps and Illustrations

MAPS

1. Bleeding Kansas and the Slavery Question   14
2. Harpers Ferry on the Eve of John Brown's Raid   24

ILLUSTRATIONS

1. Militiamen Rally to Retake Harpers Ferry, October 17, 1859   26
2. Inside the Engine House, October 18, 1859   28
3. Imagining John Brown's Last Moments, 1863   34

THE BEDFORD SERIES IN HISTORY AND CULTURE

John Brown's Raid on Harpers Ferry

A Brief History with Documents

PART ONE

Introduction:
Abolitionist, Warrior,
Martyr, Prophet

After waiting for darkness to descend on October 16, 1859, the abolitionist John Brown commenced what would be his final mission
against the institution of slavery, one that would hasten the coming of
civil war between the North and the South. That night Brown led eighteen armed men—five black and thirteen white—across the Potomac
River into the Virginia town of Harpers Ferry. Occupying the sleeping
town, even with its federal arsenal, was easy, and the men found no
resistance. The raid on Harpers Ferry was supposed to be a beginning, not an end—an opening salvo in a complex plan to carry the
abolitionists' war against slavery into the South itself. After capturing
the arsenal, Brown planned to arm slaves up and down the Appalachian Mountain chain, ignite a fierce guerilla war in the heart of the
Old South, and destroy the institution of slavery once and for all.

It didn't happen.

The slave uprising Brown hoped to inspire never materialized.
Before long, local citizens, militiamen, and U.S. troops under the command of the Virginian Robert E. Lee besieged the raiders. Brown surrendered after ten of his men, including two of his own sons, were
killed in the shootout. The raid was over in just thirty-six hours, and
Brown and six of his followers were promptly tried by the state of
Virginia, convicted, and sentenced to hang for their crimes.

While on his way to the gallows on December 2, 1859, Brown handed one of his guards a prophetic message to his countrymen, North and South: "I, John Brown, am now quite *certain* that the crimes of this *guilty land: will* never be purged *away*; but with Blood." What Brown lacked in military expertise (the raid posed only the tiniest of threats to the South) he more than made up for in his soothsaying: Harpers Ferry polarized the United States as no previous event had before, and it set in motion a dizzying spiral of actions and reactions. Whether that was its intent, the attempted insurrection struck fear into the hearts of outraged Southerners, who had long warned that abolitionists would attempt to incite a massive slave rebellion in their midst. Exaggerated reports of Brown's abolitionist network surfaced in towns large and small. At the same time, many Northerners, impressed by Brown's eloquence at his trial, shocked the South with their sympathy. Intellectuals such as Henry David Thoreau, Julia Ward Howe, and Ralph Waldo Emerson described Brown not as a madman and vigilante but as a hero. Emerson even spoke of Brown as a martyr, saying the abolitionist would make "the gallows glorious like a cross."[1]

The raid, trial, and very public death of John Brown ensured that Harpers Ferry and slavery would overshadow all issues in the 1860 presidential campaign. A year after Brown's execution, South Carolina seceded from the Union, followed by the rest of the Deep South. The Civil War that would finally destroy American slavery (and claim the lives of more than 600,000 soldiers) began six months later. Brown's role in hastening this conflict can scarcely be underestimated. He knew that by crossing into Dixie with guns and announcing he was there to free the slaves, Southern fears and anxieties would propel the nation toward cataclysm. The abortive raid thus deserves the considerable significance placed on it by contemporaries and historians alike; it is a true watershed moment in American history. There is very clearly a *before* Harpers Ferry and a starkly different *after*.

In the immediate aftermath of the raid, extremists on both sides of the slavery issue stoked public anxiety. "Southern Rights Associations" were formed to guard the border from potential marauding abolitionists, while antislavery Northerners held passionate meetings and vigils in sympathy with the raid, giving many participants a shared sense of participation in the symbolism of Harpers Ferry. Republican politicians like William H. Seward, nervously looking to the 1860 election and in fear of being tarred with Brown's radicalism, practiced their best denials and disclaimers. In New York, six thousand people attended a "Union Meeting" at the Academy of Music, where they heard old Whigs and Democrats praise manifest destiny and defend slavery as a natural blessing "decreed by nature . . . just, wise, and beneficent." The anti-Republican editor of the *New York Herald* called the meeting "the largest, the most enthusiastic, the most singular, and the most instructive meeting ever held in New York."[2]

After Brown's death, John Brown's raid became cemented in American memory, often in conflicting ways. For many Northern soldiers who marched to the song "John Brown's Body" during the Civil War, Brown's final prophecy was proof that slavery would end only with sacrificial violence and the spilling of blood. Southerners continued to revile him with almost unparalleled intensity as a braggart, a horse thief, a murderer, and an inciter of rebellion. Especially strong were the feelings African Americans had regarding John Brown. Black leaders like Frederick Douglass eulogized him, black poets like Langston Hughes memorialized him, and black intellectuals like W. E. B. Du Bois wrote heroic biographies of his life. More recently, Brown has become a hero to many of those hoping to put an end to legalized abortion in the United States. His complex legacy, clearly, marches on. But was Brown a terrorist — a nineteenth-century version of Timothy McVeigh or Osama bin Laden who murdered, for political reasons, in the name of his God? Or was he a warrior-prophet straight out of the Old Testament who committed violence only in the name of justice? In our post-9/11 world, is there any place for violence in the name of a spiritual or political cause? This collection of documents gives twenty-first-century readers a wide array of possible answers to these questions. They allow us to view the actions of men and women on both sides of the slavery issue in historical context and to recognize that their concerns continue to affect our lives a century and a half after Brown's raid. Moreover, these texts and artifacts allow readers ways to assess how actions and debates can become something larger: symbols that take on historical lives of their own.

BROWN'S EARLY LIFE

John Brown was born on May 9, 1800, in Torrington, Connecticut, in a spare, shutterless farmhouse. Although Brown's ancestors had been among the first settlers in New England and both his father and grandfather had fought in the Revolution, Brown was born into precarious circumstances. After two centuries of white settlement, land in southern New England had been divided and subdivided so many times that even eldest sons often inherited too little to sustain a family farm. This so-called man-land crisis fueled the peopling of upstate New York, the growth of cities, and the westward movement. Brown's father, Owen, a tanner, decided to move his family to Ohio's Western Reserve, hoping to farm and gain possession of enough land to pass on to his children.

Religiously, John Brown's father resembled a seventeenth-century Puritan more than the deist and free-thinking President Thomas Jefferson, who won election in the year of John Brown's birth.* Owen Brown taught each of his children to fear his austere, Calvinist God. He also taught them that slavery, which was enjoying a major resurgence in the Southern states after the invention of the labor-saving cotton gin, was a "great sin." Just as slavery was poised to explode with unprecedented speed into the fertile bottomlands of the Deep South, the young John Brown had his own first encounter with the institution and its brutality. During the War of 1812, Owen Brown won a contract to provide beef to the American forces near Detroit. Brown entrusted his twelve-year-old son with the job of gathering the cattle and driving them more than 100 miles to the army's outposts in Michigan. After one of these drives, Brown recalled lodging with a landlord who owned a "very active, intelligent, and good feeling" slave who was about his age. That night the man beat the boy with an iron shovel while the adolescent John watched in horror. He later wrote that the beating transformed him into "a most *determined Abolitionist*" from that point forward, leading him to declare an "*eternal war*" with slavery.[3]

John Brown followed his father into the tanner's trade and married an equally pious woman named Dianthe Lusk in 1820. John and Dianthe began their married life in a period of intense religious revival that historians call the "Second Great Awakening." Americans everywhere were reeling from wave after wave of social and cultural change as territorial expansion, the beginnings of the industrial revolution, and the spread of plantation slavery uprooted people and shattered old societal patterns. One reaction people had to this rapid change was to flock to evangelical religious revivals. These revival meetings were designed to produce religious conversions and led by preachers who were trained to that task. While Brown was certainly affected by the revivals, he viewed with disdain the image of a loving and forgiving

---

*As a deist, Jefferson believed that religious beliefs should be founded on human reason.

God who began to appear in the sermons of some of the more liberal Second Great Awakening preachers. Brown's God remained one of wrath and justice, more like the deity worshipped by seventeenth-century Puritans than nineteenth-century revivalists.

Brown raised his six children by Dianthe, according to one biographer, with "a rod in one hand and the Bible in the other." His attention to discipline made a powerful impression on his children. On one occasion, after punishing his son John Jr. with lashes from a "nicely-prepared blue-beech switch," he handed the whip to his son, stripped off his shirt, and ordered the boy to beat him as well, "until he received the balance" of his son's punishment. When the boy struck him, he demanded harder and harder blows until John Jr. drew blood. Only later did the son conclude his father was offering him a "practical illustration" of his belief that the innocent must also suffer for the collective guilt of sinful humankind.[4]

Dianthe died in childbirth in 1832 in New Richmond Township, Pennsylvania, where the Browns had moved in 1826 to open a tannery. Less than a year later, the thirty-three-year-old Brown married Mary Ann Day, the sixteen-year-old daughter of a local blacksmith. Mary gave birth to thirteen children during her marriage to John Brown, beginning with Sarah in 1834.

JOHN BROWN AND THE RISE OF ABOLITIONISM

As John Brown struggled to raise his family in western Pennsylvania, he was certainly aware of dramatic changes that forever shook the antislavery movement in the United States. Organized opposition to slavery during the 1810s and 1820s was essentially limited to isolated groups of free blacks, Quakers, and the American Colonization Society, founded in 1816 to bring about the gradual, voluntary (and compensated) emancipation of slaves and their "repatriation" to West Africa. In 1829 David Walker, a free black Bostonian, published his *Appeal in Four Articles*, which called for a violent overthrow of slavery and excoriated the Colonization movement for its plan to deport blacks to a continent they never knew. Walker sewed his *Appeal* into the seams of used clothing he sold to sailors, who distributed it throughout the Atlantic seaboard and helped African Americans unite in a movement for the immediate (as opposed to gradual) abolition of slavery. Walker's *Appeal* also reached white reformers like William Lloyd Garrison, a professional reformer and product of the evangelical reform culture spawned by the Second Great Awakening. On January 1, 1831, Garrison published the first issue of his newspaper *The Liberator*, in which he thundered that slavery was a national sin and demanded immediate emancipation. "I am in earnest," he said in the paper's inaugural issue. "I will not equivocate—I will not excuse—I will not retreat a single inch—AND I WILL BE HEARD!"[5]

Seven months after Garrison's clarion call, a black lay preacher in Southampton County, Virginia, named Nat Turner led the largest slave insurrection in U.S. history, killing fifty-five white men, women, and children over three bloody days. Turner's rebellion ignited an explosion of fear among southern slaveholders, who engaged in a retaliatory rampage of their own. As many as 120 African Americans, including scores of innocent victims, lost their lives as a result. Slaveholders squarely laid the blame for Turner's revolt at the feet of abolitionists like Walker and Garrison, although Garrison had never called for the violent overthrow of slavery.

It is important to note, however, that white abolitionists such as Garrison, Arthur and Lewis Tappan, Theodore Dwight Weld, and John Brown's father occupied the political fringes in antebellum America. Their antislavery activities incurred violent and often murderous responses in Southern states but also in Northern cities like Rochester, New York, and Philadelphia, where mobs raged against abolitionist agitators. Weld was known as the "most mobbed man in America," and Garrison was injured after being dragged by a rope through the streets of Boston by an anti-abolitionist mob. In 1833, Garrison and the Tappans joined forces to found the American Anti-slavery Society to coordinate petition drives, speaker's tours, sermons, newspapers, and other tracts, making abolitionism the most intense and important moral crusade in the nation's history, even as the number of its adherents remained small.

John Brown probably came to sympathize with organized abolitionism as a result of his father's influence. Owen Brown lived in Hudson, Ohio (a center for antislavery zeal), and was involved in one of the abolitionist movement's early controversies pitting radical "immediatists" (who believed in immediate uncompensated emancipation) against those who sought to end slavery gradually by colonizing West Africa with ex-slaves and free blacks. A trustee of Western Reserve College in Hudson, the elder Brown sided with the immediatist professors Beriah Green and Elizur Wright in a dispute with the large majority of colonizationists in the college community. When Green and Wright were reprimanded and a conservative president was hired, Owen

Brown resigned in disgust and transferred his support to Oberlin College, an experimental school dedicated to antiracism and coeducation.

According to family lore and one of his biographers, John Brown first read *The Liberator* at his father's house during a visit in 1833 or 1834 and soon subscribed to the paper himself. But Brown always held profound disagreements with the Garrisonians' devotion to the ideal of human perfection. Indeed, as a strict Calvinist, Brown rejected any notion that mankind (stained by original sin) could be perfected at all, a condition enjoyed by God alone. Perhaps this disagreement led to Brown's radical departure from the mainstream abolitionists regarding the use of force and violence.[6]

After encountering *The Liberator* and its stirring arguments, Brown decided to become more active in abolitionism. In the fall of 1834, Brown became convinced that God was about to bring the South's slaves "out of the house of bondage." He urged his neighbors in New Richmond to prepare to receive streams of runaways in their homes, a prospect that no doubt antagonized even his antislavery acquaintances. Brown also vowed to take a more personal role in the struggle, promising to adopt an African American boy to "give him a good English education . . . and above all, try to teach him the fear of God," and by opening a school for blacks. While he never followed through on either plan, Brown asked his brother Frederick, who also lived in Hudson, to convince some "first-rate abolitionist families" in Ohio to move to New Richmond and help finance the school. "I do honestly believe," he wrote, "that our united exertions alone might soon, with the good hand of our God upon us, effect it all."[7]

Brown's scheme to build a black schoolhouse in Pennsylvania, although visionary, was hardly practical given his finances. During the period after Dianthe's death, Brown let his tanning business slide, and he found it difficult to provide for his rapidly growing family. By the spring of 1835, he was bankrupt, and he walked away from his property in Pennsylvania to return to Ohio. There he tried his hand at land speculation, trading cattle and sheep, and, finally, opened another tannery. Each one of these business ventures failed, and a growing number of dissatisfied investors brought lawsuits against their former partner, an occurrence that became a pattern in the business life of John Brown.

As Brown brooded in Hudson, an anti-abolitionist mob in Alton, Illinois—a town just across the Mississippi from St. Louis—provided the antislavery movement with one of its most significant turning points. The antislavery editor Elijah P. Lovejoy, who had already been hounded from slaveholding Missouri for his abolitionist writings, was brutally murdered by a mob on the night of November 7, 1837. The proslavery rioters then burned his newspaper's offices and threw his printing press into the Mississippi River. Lovejoy's murder provided the abolitionists with a martyr, and public outrage broadened the antislavery movement's base in the Northern states. It also provided John Brown with a focus for his considerable energies. After listening quietly as a local scholar denounced Lovejoy's murderers in a prayer meeting in Hudson, John Brown suddenly stood up and raised his right hand. There, before a roomful of witnesses, he pledged to devote the remainder of his life to the eradication of slavery.[8]

Yet, unlike the vast majority of abolitionists—who banded together in societies, sewing circles, petition drives, and prayer groups—John Brown went his own antislavery way. He had difficulty taking orders from anyone, including his own father, and proved unwilling to listen or compromise—essential skills for working in a group. Brown became well known for berating fellow reformers for religious "errors" and supposed moral inconsistencies. His radical ideas about racial equality also set him apart from mainstream abolitionists, only a minority of whom shared his views. In 1838, for example, Brown shocked his fellow congregants by escorting visiting African Americans to sit with him in the family pew. A year later, Congregational church elders expelled the Browns, technically for being absent without reporting their whereabouts. After this incident Brown never again attended regular church services. Throughout his career he worked outside of organized resistance and reform movements.

In 1844, again on the verge of bankruptcy, Brown entered into a partnership with a wealthy Ohio businessman named Simon Perkins. Within two years, he had convinced Perkins to join him in (and finance) an ambitious venture to buy wool from shepherds throughout the northeast, grade the wool, and transport it to Springfield, Massachusetts, to command higher prices from New England buyers. After relocating to Springfield, Brown met and befriended several of the town's black citizens, many of them runaways from the South. He began to read the *North Star*, edited by the black abolitionist and one-time slave Frederick Douglass, who was drawing ever-larger crowds for his antislavery lectures. In November 1847 Douglass took time out from a lecture tour to answer Brown's invitation to discuss "urgent business" at his modest home in Springfield. After sharing a meal, Douglass recalled that Brown unfolded a weathered map of the United

States on the table and announced he had conceived a plan to liberate the nation's slaves. Running a finger up and down the Allegheny Mountains, Brown said that God had placed them there "for emancipation of the negro race." He then explained his idea for an advance force to camp in the mountains, moving up and down the chain liberating and arming the South's slaves—a plan Brown called the "Subterranean Passway." Douglass expressed doubt that Brown could evade slaveholders and their allies, who would inevitably come after him. Douglass, at this point, seemed unwilling to abandon fully the notion of convincing slaveholders to willingly free their slaves. But Brown held firm to his contention that slaveholders would never give up their property without the use of force, and Douglass conceded that his plan "had much to commend it." Upon leaving the house, Douglass wrote a letter to the *North Star* announcing his interview with Brown, who, "though a white gentleman, is in sympathy, a black man, and as deeply interested in our cause, as though his own soul had been pierced with the iron of slavery."[9]

Also while in Springfield, Brown published a bizarre essay he titled "Sambo's Mistakes" in another black abolitionist newspaper, *Ram's Horn*. In the essay Brown wrote in the voice of a free African American named Sambo who was surveying the errors of his own life in the hopes that other blacks could avoid his shortcomings. Instead of reading works of history, for example, Sambo wasted time "devouring silly novels and other miserable trash"; instead of practicing "self-denial," Sambo "bought expansive gay clothing, nice canes . . . thinking I might by that means distinguish myself from the vulgar, as some of the better class of whites do." Such essays have been part of American culture since Benjamin Franklin's alter ego, Poor Richard, began teaching generations to live frugally while also living well. But the "Sambo" character admitted to shortcomings that closely mirrored those of his creator. Although a "most zealous abolitionist," Sambo admits to having "been constantly at war with my friends about certain religious tenets." He also wasted precious time "disputing about things of no moment" and refusing to "yield any minor point of difference," resulting in the frequent necessity of acting alone. Brown finally gets to his main point in the third part of his unusual essay, when Sambo confesses to a lifetime of attempting to curry white people's favor instead of "nobly resisting their brutal aggressions from principle, and taking my place as a man." Sambo sees his rewards for this strategy as negligible indeed: the same, he says, as Northern "doughfaces" who believe themselves honored to "lick up the spittle" of a contemptuous Southern slaveholder.[10]

What was Brown's reason for publishing this strange little piece? Clearly he believed he was especially qualified to denounce American blacks for what he saw as their apathy in the face of whites' "brutal aggressions," partially out of a belief that he, almost alone among whites, was free from racial prejudice. Yet, he also felt it necessary to adopt a separate identity to avoid being seen as a white man paternalistically lecturing African Americans. In one sense Brown as author is claiming to know what was good for black people better than black people themselves. But in another, more significant sense, he was also beginning to criticize himself (and both blacks and whites in the abolitionist movement) for timidity in the face of slaveholders' aggression. Although it is relatively easy from a twenty-first-century perspective to see racial prejudice in Brown's writings and actions, it is important to note how extraordinary Brown's racial thinking was in the 1800s, even among abolitionists.

A chance meeting between Brown and a member of New England's antislavery literati at Brown's farm in the Adirondacks provides another telling example. In June 1849 the young author Richard Henry Dana Jr. (already famous for the travelogue *Two Years before the Mast*) arrived at Brown's door lost, dazed, and hungry. In his journal Dana described Brown as "a strong abolitionist and a kind of king" among the free blacks of the Adirondack outpost, noting with disapproval that he ate at the same table with black men and women and addressed his African American workers as "Mrs." and "Mr."—titles of respect. In other words, Brown treated his black neighbors as his social equals—something even the forward-thinking Dana, a founder of the antislavery Free Soil Party, found odd and unsettling.[11]

A RADICAL ABOLITIONIST

In the spring of 1848, Brown was badly in debt and facing the imminent failure of his latest business ventures. Desperate to find a way to pursue both his antislavery goals and to provide for his family, Brown turned to Gerrit Smith, an abolitionist and one of the nation's richest men. Brown had previously worked for Smith, albeit indirectly, as a surveyor of some land in western Virginia that Smith had given to Oberlin College in 1840. Now Brown heard that Smith, New York's largest landholder, had set aside 120,000 acres in the extreme northeast part of that state for free distribution to black families interested in working the land as farmers. Very few families had taken Smith up on his offer, chiefly because the land was located in the heart of the wilderness of New York's Adirondack Mountains. Brown wrote Smith a letter employing the same condescending brand of paternalism evident in "Sambo's Mistakes," offering to "take one of your farms myself, clear it up and plant it, and show my colored neighbors how much work should be done; will give them work as I have occasion, look after them in all needful ways, and be a kind of father to them." He quickly followed up the letter with a visit to Smith's estate.

When confronted by the intense, scripture-quoting (yet shabbily dressed) Brown, Smith concluded he had little to lose in taking him up on his offer. He agreed to sell Brown 244 acres on extremely favorable terms. Brown moved his family there at once and began construction of a simple farmhouse in a valley between the spectacular peaks of Whiteface and Mount Marcy, near Lake Placid and the Canadian border. Although he lived many other places, for the remainder of his life John Brown considered the Adirondack property in North Elba his home.[12]

Despite his 1839 oath to devote the rest of his life to the eradication of slavery, Brown continued to pursue a series of increasingly desperate business ventures. One of these took the form of an ill-conceived trip to Europe to sell wool amassed during his partnership with Simon Perkins. The scheme, like most of Brown's business forays, proved disastrous. He and his partner lost approximately $40,000, and Perkins & Brown faced a mountain of lawsuits. It was at this point that Brown took another step in his metamorphosis from an abolitionist-businessman to a full-fledged crusader for the rights of African Americans.

This transformation was prompted by external political events, such as the war with Mexico—which added hundreds of thousands of miles of new territory to the United States—and the Compromise of 1850, which attempted to "solve," once and for all, the controversy over whether that territory would remain free or be open to slavery. To Brown and many other abolitionists, the Compromise was a massive capitulation to slaveholders and their allies. Despite the admission to the Union of California as a free state and the abolition of the slave trade (but not slavery) in the District of Columbia, the abolitionists were mostly correct in this assumption. By far the most significant part of the Compromise was the new Fugitive Slave Law, the principal demand of the slaveholding South. A massive expansion of federal power at the expense of the states, the law placed the federal government and law enforcement agencies squarely on the side of slaveholders in search of their runaways. The sight of federal marshals and slave catchers on the streets of Philadelphia, Boston, or even North Elba incensed abolitionists and even larger numbers of more moderate Northerners. A fugitive in chains being returned to slavery and the South personalized the issue and made it real for thousands of Northerners for whom, up to this point, slavery had been a hazy abstraction. For an already committed abolitionist like John Brown, the new law was an abomination.

In the wake of a well-publicized case of a runaway being returned to slavery in 1851, Brown composed a manifesto and presented it to a group of free black friends in Springfield, Massachusetts. Entitled "Words of Advice: Branch of the United States League of Gileadites" (Document 1), Brown's essay urged African Americans to band together to resist the Fugitive Slave Law and all who sought to enforce it—even to the point of killing slavecatchers. "Be firm, detached, and cool," Brown wrote, "stand by one another and by your friends, while a drop of blood remains; and be hanged, if you must, but tell no tales out of school. Make no confession."[13] Taking a page from the African American abolitionist Henry Highland Garnet (who preached slave rebellion), Brown attempted to foment an armed resistance against the Fugitive Slave Law. Inspired by what they heard, forty-four black men and women in Springfield joined Brown's United League of the Gileadites. Without Brown's presence, however, the group took little action.

Brown spent much of the next three years fighting his various lawsuits and trying in vain to save his wool business. By 1854 he was exhausted and penniless, and his reputation as a businessman (with fifteen different failures in four states) was in tatters. It is anyone's guess what John Brown might have done next if it had not been for the introduction of the Kansas-Nebraska Act and the reemergence of slavery as a central focus in American political life. By opening up land for white settlement in the former Louisiana Purchase that had, since 1821, been marked out as free soil, the federal government ensured that economic and political interests would collide in what was coming to be known as Kansas. When it was made clear that the people who settled the new territories would be allowed to decide whether to allow slavery there, that collision was almost guaranteed to turn violent. The race for the "virgin soil" of Kansas was on, and Brown's experiences there would change him and the abolitionist movement forever. (See Map 1.)

MAKING KANSAS BLEED

Even before the Kansas-Nebraska Act became law, settlers from each side of the slavery issue streamed into the territory's fertile river valleys. They came for a multitude of reasons, ranging from self-interested economic ambition to unbridled ideological passion. More than a few combined the two. As a rule, settlers from nearby Missouri, a slave state, and the rest of the South wanted to mark out the territory for slavery, whereas those coming from the free states of New England and upstate New York sought to ban the institution. Arrivals from the newer states of Indiana, Illinois, and Iowa tended to concentrate on the economic benefits and prospects for land ownership.

The Kansas-Nebraska Act was the brainchild of the Illinois Senator Stephen A. Douglas, known as the "Little Giant" for his diminutive size, oratorical skills (later utilized in the famous debates against Abraham Lincoln in 1858), and legislative prowess. Specifically, the bill sought to organize territory in the Louisiana Purchase north of present-day Oklahoma to pave the way for a transcontinental railroad linking the gold fields in California to Chicago and the East. Many Americans viewed the organization of this territory for future statehood as long overdue, but each addition of new territory to the United States inevitably inflamed the controversy over whether the lands would allow slavery or remain free soil, with each struggle seemingly a greater threat to the Union than the last.[14]

The last major attempt to calm the tensions over slavery, the four-year-old Compromise of 1850, failed completely to satisfy either side. And Southern senators, arguing that slavery in Missouri would be endangered if it was surrounded on three sides by free territory, wanted an end to the exclusion—a result of the Missouri Compromise of 1821—of slavery from any territory carved from the Louisiana Purchase north of 36°30′ (roughly the Arkansas-Missouri border). Douglas, who knew he would need Southern support if he wanted to win the 1856 Democratic presidential nomination, gave the Southern senators exactly what they wanted. He proposed to divide the new territory in two, with Nebraska Territory encompassing the modern states of Nebraska, the Dakotas, and Montana, and Kansas

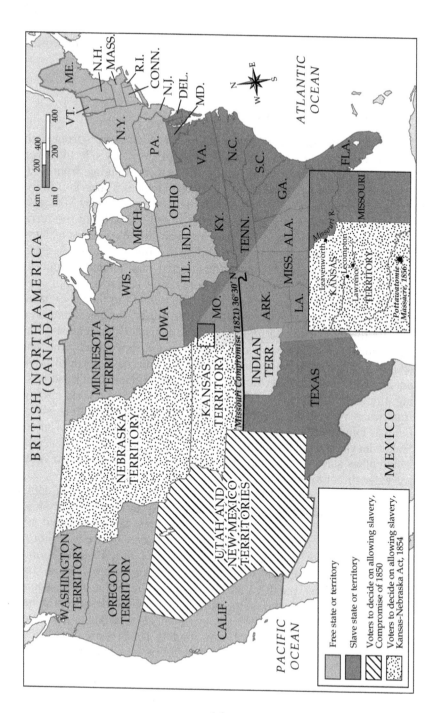

Territory the land within the state's current boundaries and some of what eventually became Colorado.

For many Northerners like the Browns, the meaning of Douglas's legislation was clear: Kansas, the more southern of the two territories, was to be marked out for slavery, a refutation of the Missouri Compromise. Douglas himself, a believer in "Popular Sovereignty"—letting a territory's settlers decide for or against slavery—famously claimed to "care not" whether the settlers in the new territories voted slavery up or down, as long as "the tide of immigration and civilization" were permitted to roll onward.

But thousands of Americans—including John Brown and his huge family—*did* care. When it became clear that southerners had the votes in Congress to pass the Kansas-Nebraska Act, the New York Whig William H. Seward stood up on the floor of the Senate and told his Southern colleagues, "Since there is no escaping your challenge, I accept it in behalf of the cause of freedom. We will engage in competition for the virgin soil of Kansas, and God give victory to the side which is stronger in numbers as it is in right." The race for Kansas was on, and the Brown family was in the thick of it from the very beginning. It was a defining moment for the Browns and the nation.[15]

In the weeks after the passage of the Kansas-Nebraska Act on May 25, 1854, Missouri residents used their proximity to outpace free-state emigration to the new territory of Kansas. But as the year 1854 wore on, settlers from the North first equaled, and then surpassed, Southern numbers. It was during that summer that John Brown's son John Brown Jr. decided to emigrate and stake a claim in Kansas—like many others on both the pro- and antislavery sides—to become a farmer there as well as a soldier on the front lines of the battle over slavery and its expansion. Brown's sons Jason, Owen, Frederick, and Salmon, ranging in age from eighteen to thirty-three, agreed to join him, as did Samuel Adair, the elder Brown's brother-in-law. At first

---

Map 1. *Bleeding Kansas and the Slavery Question*
The addition of new territory (such as that seized from Mexico after the 1846–1848 war) sparked acrimonious debate between North and South over whether new lands would be slave or free. Both the Compromise of 1850 (which admitted California as a free state, potentially opened New Mexico and Utah to slavery, and enacted a federal Fugitive Slave Law) and the Kansas-Nebraska Act of 1854 (which opened up territory formerly marked out for free soil to slaveholders) escalated tensions and led John Brown to the center of the disputes.

John Brown Sr. declined to join the party, writing his son that he felt "committed to operate in another part of the field." He added that if he "were not so committed, I would be on my way this fall."[16] By May of 1855, however, Brown had changed his mind. He had received a long letter from John Jr. asking for help procuring weapons for the fight against proslavery settlers and "border ruffians." "The friends of freedom are not one fourth of them half armed, and as to Military Organization among them it no where exists in this territory," the son wrote to his father. The letter struck exactly the right chord for the abolitionist who had planned to confront the slave power with violence, if necessary. John Brown left for Kansas soon after, leaving behind Mary and a new baby—Ellen, his twentieth child—in North Elba. He also left behind numerous lawsuits and business entanglements in Ohio, Massachusetts, and Great Britain for a new life as a full-time soldier in the war against slavery, one that would stretch from his departure for Kansas to his descent from the gallows in Virginia four years later.[17]

The old man was shocked at what he found when he arrived in October 1855 at the rude settlement on North Middle Creek that his sons had named Brown's Station. Most of the family was debilitated with fever, "shivering over their little fires, all exposed to the dreadful cutting winds." Brown and his son-in-law quickly sprang into action, building structures, bringing in the meager harvest of beans and squash, and chopping wood for the coming Kansas winter. The elder Brown's arrival almost certainly saved the family's western experiment from immediate disaster.[18]

Despite the continuing hardships of frontier life, antislavery politics was a constant factor for the Browns, even during the difficult months of late 1855. The previous March, proslavery Missourians had illegally crossed the state line in droves to elect a proslavery territorial legislature (labeled the "bogus legislature" by members of the emerging free-state majority). The legislature convened in July and passed a draconian legal code that essentially outlawed antislavery action, thought, and speech. The territorial code (Document 2) stipulated that only proslavery men would be allowed to hold office and serve on juries and outlined severe punishments for speaking out against slavery (five years at hard labor), helping runaway slaves escape (ten years in prison), and possessing books about slave rebellion or fomenting insurrection (death by hanging). To combat the "bogus legislature," free-state settlers, including John Brown Jr., met in a separate convention to create an alternate (and antislavery) constitution for Kansas.

Almost immediately after the elder Brown's arrival in late 1855, the residents of Brown's Station received word that a proslavery Virginian had murdered a free-state settler after a dispute. This emboldened citizens in the antislavery town of Lawrence, thirty miles north of Brown's Station, to hold a protest meeting, where they agreed to take up arms. The proslavery county sheriff and governor, informed that an armed force in Lawrence was in "open rebellion" against the laws of the territory, mobilized the militia and invited back the "border ruffians" who had fraudulently swung the election the previous spring. A large and rowdy mob gathered on the banks of the Wakarusa River south of Lawrence, spoiling for a fight.

The Browns, armed to the teeth, arrived in Lawrence on December 7, at one point marching straight through a crowd of Missourians to cross the bridge into town. As soon as they arrived at the Free State Hotel, the fortress-like headquarters of the Lawrence free staters, the elder Brown was commissioned as a "captain" in the First Brigade of Kansas Volunteers and given command of a small company (mostly consisting of his own sons) called the Liberty Guards. The Guards saw little action that day, since the governor was able to broker a deal whereby the increasingly intoxicated Missourians massing on the edge of Lawrence would retreat and the free-state leaders would announce they had no intention of resisting the laws of the territory. Violence in Lawrence was, for the moment, averted (Document 3).

The bitter Kansas winter briefly quelled the tensions of the previous fall. But the convening of the competing, free-state government in Topeka in March 1856 again brought the situation to a boiling point. Word reached Brown's Station on May 22, 1856, that yet another crowd of border ruffians had assembled at the Missouri line, planning to attack the free-state stronghold of Lawrence. Brown and his Liberty Guards quickly armed themselves, mounted their horses, and left for Lawrence just after midnight on May 23. They were too late: The Missourians had already sacked the town, leveling the Free State Hotel with a barrage of artillery shells and tossing abolitionist printing presses into the river.[19]

Brown was anxious to avenge the sack of Lawrence, but he also may have received news that morning about a vicious attack on the antislavery Senator Charles Sumner by Congressman Preston Brooks in the U.S. Senate. Brooks had beaten Sumner unconscious with a heavy cane in anger over a speech the Massachusetts senator had delivered about Kansas that included personal attacks on Brooks's uncle, a senator from South Carolina. Years later Brown's son Salmon recalled that a messenger had brought the news and that Brown and his brothers had gone "crazy — *crazy*. It seemed to be the finishing, decisive touch." While Sumner's Kansas speech was tinged with self-righteousness and insult, Brown's words more exactly matched those of his Southern foes. "We must fight fire with fire," Brown said, according to one of his followers. "Something must be done to show these barbarians that we, too, have rights."[20]

The result was another act of horrific violence — and a transformative one for Brown. Leading four of his sons and three others to a proslavery settlement at nearby Pottawatomie Creek that same night, Brown's men dragged five settlers from their cabins and split open their heads with broadswords (Document 4). Controversy still surrounds the killings that came to be known as the Pottawatomie Massacre, much of it stemming from the fact that John Brown never formally confessed to his role in the murders. The dead men owned no slaves, nor had they participated in the assault on Lawrence. Most observers could agree on two facts, however: The murders and the exhaustive newspaper coverage made John Brown a legend and a household name — in the North as well as the South — and they guaranteed that Kansas would continue to "bleed" profusely in 1856.[21]

Although most other free staters condemned the massacre, Brown's adoption of violence gave voice to the rage and despair many free-state Kansans experienced during the fifteen months after the election that created the "bogus" legislature. Coming so soon after the sack of Lawrence, the murders helped spur formerly peaceful settlers to act with force, even as their political leaders called for calm and negotiation. "Violence breeds violence," wrote James Hanway, who was shocked at the murders but continued to support Brown and condemn the proslavery party. "They advocate assassination and now that five persons have been murdered on their side perhaps they will learn that such hellish sentiments when carried into effect, will work equally to the destruction of proslavery men."[22]

This new feeling of defiance and opposition led many free-state settlers — most of whom condemned the Pottawatomie murders — nevertheless to gather their weapons and take to the brush for out-and-out battle with the proslavery side. Leading the way was John Brown, whose legend was growing fast. He was now an outlaw with a price on his head and federal troops, vigilantes, and crowds of Missourians in constant pursuit. Brown's guerilla band initially hid out near Ottawa Creek and was the subject of a colorful description by the Scottish-born reporter James Redpath: "A dozen horses were tied, all ready saddled for a ride for life, or a hunt after Southern invaders. A dozen rifles and sabers were stacked around the trees . . . and two fine-looking youths were standing, leaning on their arms, on guard near by." Brown "stood near the fire, with his shirt-sleeves rolled up, and a large piece of pork in his hand. . . . He was poorly clad, and his toes protruded from his boots."[23]

The battles of Black Jack (where Brown, now a wanted man and outnumbered two to one, captured the man deputized to catch him) and Osawatomie in June and August of 1856, sealed John Brown's fame as a fearsome guerilla fighter.[24] Brown continued to evade capture, but a force of 250 men killed his son Frederick and burned the free-state town of Osawatomie to the ground. His son Jason later recalled that, while watching the flames, his father said, "God sees it. I have only a short time to live—only one death to die, and I will die fighting this cause. There will be no more peace in this land until slavery is done for. I will give them something else to do than to extend slave territory. I will carry the war into Africa." By "Africa" Brown meant that he would next attack slavery where slavery already existed: in the South itself.[25]

More than fifty people died in the convulsions of violence that historians call Bleeding Kansas in 1856 (although some historians believe the number was far higher). Not until President Pierce sent a new territorial governor and 1,300 federal troops to Kansas in September did the violence subside. Brown, ill with dysentery and pursued by scores of bounty hunters and federal marshals, slipped out of Kansas and headed east via Nebraska in October. He promised his wife, Mary, that he would return to the territory "if the troubles continue and my health will admit." Meanwhile, John Brown had other plans for his war against slavery.

THE PLAN

Brown was transformed by his Kansas experience. The failed businessman had emerged from his time in the territory as a famous man of action, brimming with ideas for future assaults on what he called the "sin of slavery." Despite being wanted for murder and other crimes, the newly minted celebrity spent the first ten months of 1857 raising money in New England to fund further Kansas escapades (Document 5). It was during this time that he also began updating his plan to attack slavery in the South by means of a "Subterranean passway" in the Appalachians. While in Boston, Brown won an important convert to his cause: a young Harvard graduate and school-teacher named Franklin Sanborn. Sanborn was almost immediately in awe of the charismatic, tanned, and heavily armed warrior from Kansas. In addition to offering his help raising and arming a company of men, Sanborn introduced his new hero to a group of influential Boston abolitionists who would be instrumental in funding Brown's schemes. Sanborn and five others—businessman George L. Stearns, Worcester pastor Thomas Wentworth Higginson, Dr. Samuel Gridley Howe, the Reverend Theodore Parker, and the New York philanthropist Gerrit Smith—became known as the "Secret Six" for their covert effort to funnel money and weapons to Brown.

The old man returned to Kansas in November 1857 to recruit his fighting force. The fighters, who included John H. Kagi, John E. Cook, Aaron Stevens, C. P. Tidd, and William H. Leeman, were at first shocked when told they would not be fighting border ruffians in Kansas. Their next stop was Tabor, Iowa, where Brown had been stockpiling Sharpe's rifles, revolvers, ammunition, and more than one thousand pikes (long-handled weapons with double-edged blades). After transporting the cache to Chambersburg, Pennsylvania, Brown left his group there to train under the tutelage of a down-and-out English soldier of fortune and fencing instructor named Hugh Forbes.

Brown's experiences in Kansas had led to a significant change in his strategy to end slavery: instead of encouraging slaves to flee into the mountains or Canada to make slave property less secure, he now planned for the rapid establishment of a free, biracial state in the midst of the Old South. The new "free state" could then be used as a staging area for further missions to disrupt slavery from within. First, however, Brown decided he needed to create a system of laws for the new mountain state. He traveled to Frederick Douglass's hometown of Rochester to visit the abolitionist and work on the "Provisional Constitution and Ordinances for the People of the United States" (Document 7). Dedicated to the "oppressed"—people who after the *Dred Scott* decision* were "declared to have no rights which the white man is bound to respect"—the constitution set up a government with a president, a unicameral assembly, a court system of elected judges, and a citizenry of farmer-soldiers. All property in the free state was to

---

Dred Scott v. Sandford, decided by the U.S. Supreme Court in 1857, ruled that Congress had no authority to regulate slavery in the territories and that people of African descent are not citizens of the United States.

be held in common. Furthermore, slaveholders' property was to be "confiscated and taken, whenever and wherever it may be found, in either free or slave states."[26]

Brown then laid out his plan to a select group of supporters in Peterboro, New York, "to the astonishment and almost dismay of those present." The audacity of the plan was impressive, but the details were extremely sketchy. Assuming Brown succeeded in establishing his Appalachian stronghold (a big assumption indeed), how would the free state defend itself from the inevitable force of the states and federal government? Brown brushed aside the questions with the peculiar combination of extreme self-confidence and Old Testament–style righteousness that made him such a mesmerizing figure. As Sanborn wrote, "Without accepting Brown's plans as reasonable, we were prepared to second them merely because they were his."[27]

Brown's next task was to present his plan and provisional constitution to the African American community and win its support. For this he traveled to Chatham, Ontario, a haven for runaway American slaves forty-five miles east of Detroit. Joined by his fighting force and the famous black abolitionist Martin R. Delany, Brown told the assembled group that slaves all over the South were ready to revolt and claim their freedom. As soon as a strong leader was sent to liberate them and "upon the first intimation of a plan formed for [their liberation]," the slaves "would immediately rise all over the Southern states." Brown offered himself as that leader.[28]

Then, in front of the hushed and, more than likely, skeptical crowd, Brown for the first time publicly revealed his plan for a direct attack on slavery. He proposed to raise an armed band, invade the South somewhere in the Blue Ridge Mountains, and then wage a guerilla slave rebellion in the mountains of western Virginia, North Carolina, Tennessee, and northern Alabama. As he moved along the mountain chain, he predicted, thousands of slaves would swarm to his side, ready to wage war on the plantations on both sides of the Appalachians. What's more, he predicted that "all the free Negroes in the Northern states" and Canada would immediately rally to aid the invaders once word got out, and his victorious biracial force would then set up a new constitutional republic in the conquered territory of the Old South. Once the momentous free state was firmly established, the surrounding states would be forced to emancipate their slaves and the institution would collapse under its own weight.

For some time after Brown finished, no one spoke. Finally, someone asked, "But what if troops are brought against you?" Brown dismissed the questioner with a wave of the hand and a touch of military bravado. A small, well-disciplined force could easily defend the ravines of western Virginia against even the best Southern soldiers, he assured his audience, comparing the topography of the Blue Ridge to the Thermopylae, a famed mountain pass in Greece where Leonides held off Xerxes during the Persian Wars. Besides, he said, he had been specially chosen as God's instrument for such an expedition, and it was God's will that slavery be eradicated with the blood of slaveholders.

It is testament to Brown's strength as a communicator that his plan and his "Provisional Constitution" were adopted with only minimal changes (most debate centered on an Article that declared that the Provisional Constitution in no way encouraged the overthrow of any state government of the United States). Brown objected to the suggestion that the struggle against slavery was a struggle against the United States. He sought the nation's salvation, he argued, not its destruction. Slaveholders were traitors, not freedom fighters.[29]

With the plan hatched, Brown made a final return to Kansas, where he led a daring rescue of eleven Missouri slaves. The eighty-two-day (and more than 1,000-mile) wintry journey to freedom in Canada only added to Brown's mystique as an abolitionist avenger (Document 6). He spent the late spring of 1859 saying goodbye to his family in North Elba. Then he traveled to western Maryland, where he rented a small farm just across the Potomac River from Harpers Ferry. He assembled his men, transported the weapons, and proceeded to make the activities at the farm look as normal as possible. As the summer days shortened into autumn, Brown finally revealed his plan to the motley group of warriors he had assembled. It was the second surprise he had sprung on them. First, he had decided to abandon "Bleeding Kansas" and work instead to establish a free state in the Appalachians from which to run off slaves. Now he announced that they would begin by attacking and seizing a federal arsenal. Once more, John Brown had to face down dissenters in his own ranks, and once again—with a combination of careful explanation and personal reassurances—he was successful. Such were his powers of persuasion.

Brown still had one more person he wanted to convince to fight at his side. He slipped away from the farm to meet Frederick Douglass at a stone quarry near Chambersburg, where he informed his old friend of his plan to attack Harpers Ferry. "Come with me, Douglass.... When I strike, the bees will begin to swarm, and I shall want you to help hive them," he said. Douglass recalled that, although moved by the old man's eloquence, he still believed the plan was folly. What began as a plan to bleed the South of its black labor had become a scheme to, with one outrageous act, awaken the nation to the evils of slavery. After opposing Brown's assertions "with all the arguments I could command," Douglass declined to join the mission. His traveling companion, a free black named Shields Green, chose otherwise. Douglass returned to Rochester alone, and Green stayed to fight alongside John Brown.[30]

Two months later, at eight o'clock on October 16, Brown left his son Owen and two other recruits to guard the supplies at the rented farmhouse and led his remaining seventeen comrades into the autumn night (see Map 2).

THE RAID

The raiding party was an unusual one, to be sure. Contained within its ranks were free blacks, runaway slaves, elite white college men, and utopian idealists. The ages of the raiders ranged from twenty to Brown's fifty-nine, although with his iconic billowing beard he looked much older. Each was strong in his abolitionism and fully in John Brown's sway. At approximately ten o'clock, the raiders crossed the Potomac River Bridge, captured its night watchman, and cut the telegraph wires. They then proceeded to the armory, where they quickly overpowered the lone guard and placed him, along with their other prisoner, in the engine house, a small fire station adjacent to the armory's gate. With the armory safely in the raiders' hands, Brown turned his sights on the other "targets" of the sleeping town: the arsenal, the bridge over the Shenandoah, and the Hall rifle works on a small island south of town. A small party traveled west to local plantations to capture slaveholders and proclaim to the slaves that their deliverance had begun. The first hours of John Brown's raid were both methodical and extremely successful.

But big trouble was on the way. First, a relief watchman arrived to take his post at the Potomac Bridge, noticed it was unguarded, and ran to the Wager House hotel near the railroad station to sound the alarm. A baggage handler and slave named Hayward Shepherd ironically became the antislavery raid's first fatality when he ventured to the bridge to check on the situation and was shot. At about 1 a.m. on October 17, a hotel employee passed word to the conductor of an eastbound train on the Baltimore & Ohio Railroad that an armed party had taken over the bridge. John Brown emerged to talk with the con-

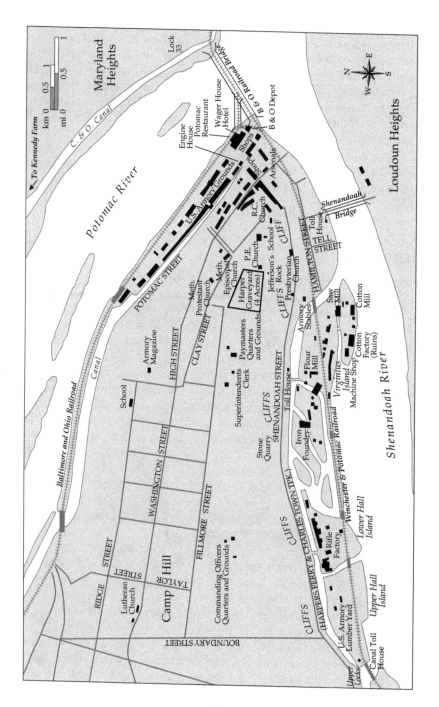

24

ductor himself and, fatefully, permitted the train's passage to Baltimore. No sooner had he crossed the bridge than the conductor lit up the telegraph wires with news—faulty and overblown news, to be sure—that a "Negro insurrection" had been accomplished at Harpers Ferry, arms had been disbursed to local slaves, and 150 raiders held the town hostage. John Brown had been granted his wish to make big news with the raid, yet instead of taking to the hills with weapons and freed slaves from local plantations, he returned to the engine house to wait for his army of newly emancipated reinforcements. They never came.

As dawn broke on Monday, October 17, church bells rang out across Jefferson County, warning of an invasion and alerting local militiamen that their services were required. By noon two companies had arrived on the outskirts of town, still unsure what kind of attack they had been called in to repel (Figure 1). About 1 p.m. at the Shenandoah Bridge, militiamen from Charles Town shot and killed the raider Dangerfield Newby, a forty-four-year-old ex-slave from Virginia who had hoped to free his wife and children. Townspeople and militiamen then surrounded the rifle works, guarded by Brown's second-in-command, John H. Kagi, and two free black Ohioans, John Anthony Copeland and Lewis Sheridan Leary. The three fled by jumping from a window into the river, where Kagi and Leary were fatally shot and Copeland was captured. Worse still for the raiders, the men who were sent with supplies and weapons to join Owen and the other guards back at the farm were apprehended. This left John Brown, a handful of raiders, and their approximately thirty captives in the tiny engine house with no means of escape. Brown's attempts to arrange a truce under a white flag were met with bullets—one of which mortally wounded his son Watson and another a young recruit named Aaron Stevens.

After a raider shot and killed the mayor of Harpers Ferry from the engine house, the townsfolk responded with vindictive violence. Willie

---

Map 2. *Harpers Ferry on the Eve of John Brown's Raid*

In 1859 Harpers Ferry was a bustling town located at the confluence of the Potomac and Shenandoah rivers, home to a federal armory and arsenal. John Brown and his raiders crossed the Potomac after nightfall on October 16, quickly captured the federal armory, and took hostages to the engine house. Next, the raiders secured the arsenal and rifle factory on nearby Hall Island. On October 17 local militiamen attacked and killed seven raiders and trapped Brown, his men, and their hostages in the engine house. The next day U.S. marines stormed the engine house, captured Brown, and put an end to the raid.

National Park Service, *Guide to John Brown's Raid*, 1973.

EN ROUTE FOR HARPER'S FERRY.—[SKETCHED BY PORTE CRAYON.]

Figure 1. *Militiamen Rally to Retake Harpers Ferry, October 17, 1859*

This image by David Strother (usually known by his nom de plume "Porte Crayon") was part of the flood of news coverage that followed in the wake of Brown's raid on Harpers Ferry. By coincidence Strother was in nearby Charles Town at the start of the raid and claimed to be an eyewitness to the events of October 17 and 18.

Harper's Weekly, November 26, 1859.

Leeman, at twenty the youngest raider, was shot at point-blank range while trying to escape, and William Thompson, held captive at the Wager House hotel, was dragged to the river and riddled with bullets. His body was left floating in the shallows. Late Monday evening, a complement of U.S. Marines, led by Brevet Colonel Robert E. Lee and his aide Lieutenant J. E. B. Stuart, arrived at the armory gates. Early on the morning of October 18, Stuart passed a note from Lee to Brown through a crack in the engine house door, calling for immediate and unconditional surrender. When Brown refused, the marines began their assault on the building. Within a few minutes it was all over: the marines stormed the building, killed two more raiders, and took the others prisoner. Brown, wounded with sword injuries to his head and shoulder, was immediately taken to a nearby office (Figure 2). Of the twenty-two men involved in the raid, ten of Brown's men (including his sons Watson and Oliver) were dead or mortally wounded, and five, including Brown, were captured. Two others were later captured, and just five—Owen Brown, Osborne Perry Anderson, Barclay Coppoc, Francis Jackson Merriam, and Charles Plummer Tidd—escaped with their lives (Document 8).

Within hours of Brown's evacuation to the paymaster's office, important visitors arrived from Washington, Richmond, and elsewhere. Each peppered the wounded man with angry questions about his weapons, his Provisional Constitution, his source of funds, and his reasons for staging the raid. He answered them all, and reporters raptly recorded every word of the exchanges (Document 9). The abolitionist who became a warrior in Kansas was beginning his final transformation into a martyr. "We came to free the slaves, and only that," Brown told one questioner. "You had better—" he went on, "all you people of the South—prepare yourselves for a settlement of this question. . . . You may dispose of me very easily—I am nearly disposed of now; but this question is still to be settled—this negro question I mean; the end of that is not yet."[31]

THE TRIAL

John Brown's eloquence posed a much graver threat to slavery and the South than his skills as a military leader. And during his rushed trial, he had a virtual army of reporters copying down his every utterance.

The day after his capture, John Brown and the other raiders in custody were moved to Charles Town, the Jefferson County seat eight

JOHN BROWN AT HARPER'S FERRY.

Figure 2. *Inside the Engine House, October 18, 1859*
This wood engraving by Alfred Bobbett (after an illustration by Felix O. C. Darley) dates from the 1870s and took readers inside the engine house during the last moments of John Brown's siege of Harpers Ferry on October 18, 1859. Intending to make Brown appear heroic, the artist placed the old man in the center of the picture, nursing a fallen comrade (perhaps his own son Oliver, who died from his wounds) and issuing orders to the multi-racial raiding party. Unlike Figure 1, this engraving was not based on an eyewitness account.
The Granger Collection, New York.

miles from Harpers Ferry. The wounded old man had to be carried into the courtroom for a preliminary hearing on October 25 and the trial itself two days later. Efforts to delay the hearing until Brown's lawyer could be present were overruled. One reason for the haste was Virginia authorities' desire to try and convict Brown before angry

Southerners, who were pouring into the tiny town by the trainload, could lynch him. They also justifiably feared that excited abolitionists might try to help their hero break out of jail. Honor-driven Virginians like Governor Henry Wise could not bear the thought of their prisoner recruiting still more volunteers on the streets of Northern cities. But John Brown did not desire escape: he had his eyes on a much grander prize. He outlined his new thinking in a letter to his wife: "I can recover all the lost capital occasioned by that disaster by only hanging a few moments by the neck; and I feel quite determined to make the utmost possible out of a defeat." This was precisely what he did.[32]

Brown's first act as his trial began was to shout down a lawyer retained by one of the Secret Six who tried to present an insanity defense. A recurrent explanation for Brown's raid, especially in the South, was the abolitionist's supposed insanity, a theme adopted by several of Brown's biographers over the years. Some authors have gone so far as to rest their cases on Brown's facial expressions in photographs and recreated medical "family trees" to diagnose his presumedly addled mental state. Yet although Brown's behavior and actions were clearly obsessive, few people who knew him well questioned his sanity. As David Reynolds noted in a recent biography, the raid reflected Brown's overconfidence in white people's ability to rise above racism and black people's willingness to rise against their masters in armed insurrection more than any lack of sanity or reason.[33] In any case, Brown understood that any defense that rested on his lack of sanity would obscure his larger arguments about the sins of slavery. "I reject, so far as I am capable," he thundered from his cot in the courtroom, "any attempt to interfere on my behalf on that score. If I am insane . . . I should think I know more than all the rest of the world" (Document 10).

Instead of an insanity defense, Brown's lawyers chose to attack the leading charge against him: treason against the state of Virginia. This charge continues to strike many observers as odd, since Brown's attack was on a U.S. armory and he admitted to attempting to incite rebellion, both federal (not state) offenses. The willingness of the administration of President James Buchanan to allow Virginia to try Brown, which would almost certainly result in a death sentence, reveals an important point about the supercharged atmosphere of sectionalism surrounding the case. By "handing over" Brown to Virginia, the federal government was hoping to pacify Southerners and to minimize the chances of retributive violence. Brown's lawyers called as witnesses Harpers Ferry hostages in an attempt to prove Brown did not intend to harm them, only to free area slaves. But such arguments proved useless. On October 31, just four days after the trial began and after only forty-five minutes of deliberation, the jury pronounced John Brown guilty of treason against Virginia, murder, and inciting slave rebellion.[34]

Three days later Brown was back in court for sentencing. He asked to speak, and in a short five minutes delivered what his biographer Oswald Garrison Villard accurately called "some of the most stirring words ever to come from an American courtroom." After disingenuously arguing that he never intended murder, treason, or the destruction of property, Brown turned to the larger question at hand. Declaring that the Bible's Golden Rule forced him to act as he did, Brown said the following:

> I believe that to have interfered as I have done in behalf of His despised poor, is no wrong, but right. Now, if it is deemed necessary that I should forfeit my life for the furtherance of the ends of justice, and mingle my blood with the blood of millions in this slave country whose rights are disregarded by wicked, cruel, and unjust enactments, I say let it be done.

The judge listened patiently to Brown's oration before sentencing him to hang on December 2. But thousands of Northerners who read the speech in their newspapers were strongly affected by the old man's moral clarity. Where Southerners saw a traitor and a murderer, more and more Northerners began to see a great and good man sacrificing his life for the cause of liberty—to right the American paradox that guaranteed slavery in a land dedicated to freedom.[35]

Brown spent the last month of his life working to cement his legacy as an abolitionist martyr (Document 11). The Virginia authorities inadvertently aided in Brown's "canonization" by allowing him to correspond freely and receive visitors, and the condemned man did not waste a single moment. He composed a dizzying number of letters to family and friends, many of which quickly wound up in print. The overweening emotion this month's correspondence elicited—from even Brown's staunchest opponents—was sympathy and respect for the bravery with which he faced death. One jailer who was obliged to read the outgoing mail recalled having to wipe away tears as he made his way through the pile of eloquent missives. "Your most cheering letter of the 27th of Oct. is received," he wrote to one correspondent on November 1. "You know that Christ once armed Peter. So in my case, I think he put a sword in my hand, and there it continued, so long as he saw best, and then kindly took it from me. . . . I wish you could know with what cheerfulness I am now wielding the 'Sword of the Spirit' on the right hand and on the left. I bless God that it proves 'mighty to the pulling down of strongholds.'"[36] Brown's mission was aided by a truly remarkable group of journalists, who vividly reported on every detail of his last month on earth, and visitors, who wrote of the condemned man's nobility during his last days. "He could form beautiful dreams of things, as they should occur," recalled Mrs. Thomas Russell fifty years after the raid, "and forwith go into action on the basis of those dreams. . . . John Brown's dreams were not always practical. But we loved and trusted *John Brown*."[37]

In the South, of course, reactions to Brown were markedly different. Virginia governor Henry Wise received mailbags full of letters advising the best course for what to do with John Brown (including one from a man claiming to be a professor of anatomy asking for Brown's actual *head* for his collection and another urging dissection be part of the punishment for the raid). "The rage for vengeance which is felt by the citizens of this place can only be fully and satisfactorily satisfied by the blood of John Brown," wrote the fire-eating* editor of the Charleston *Mercury*.[38] Despite the ghoulish requests, Wise granted permission for Mary Brown to claim her husband's body and bury it in North Elba. On the morning of December 2, Brown rode atop his own coffin to the gallows, in full view of the crowd and the hundreds of soldiers President Buchanan had ordered to Charles Town to keep the peace. Among them were many men who would become household names in the Civil War era: Professor Thomas J. ("Stonewall") Jackson, later a general in the Confederate army, who brought along cadets from the Virginia Military Institute; the fire-eater Edmund Ruffin, who would later pull the lanyard that began the bombardment of Fort Sumter and commenced the war; and John Wilkes Booth, at the time a famous actor but known today for assassinating Abraham Lincoln in 1865. Brown handed one of his jailers a prophetic note containing his last message to a riveted public: "I, John Brown, am now quite *certain* that the crimes of this *guilty land: will* never be purged *away*; but with Blood. I had *as I now think vainly* flattered myself that without *very much* bloodshed; it might be done." After riding to the gallows and ascending the platform, the sheriff cut

---

*Fire-eaters were Southern extremists who advocated secession in the years before the Civil War.

the rope, and Brown dropped through with a loud crash. A spectator recalled, "There was very little motion of his person for several moments, and soon the wind blew his lifeless body to and fro." Six days later John Brown was buried on his North Elba farm overlooking Mount Tahawus in the Adirondacks.[39]

RECKONING WITH JOHN BROWN

During the winter of 1859–1860, John Brown's raid, trial, and execution promoted a sense of crisis and panic in both sections of the country. Southerners hastily convened vigilance committees and military companies to put down expected abolitionist incursions. Reports of random and unprovoked violence against Northerners came in from across the region. These developments strengthened the hand of Southern fire-eaters who were eager for secession and cited the raid as proof that abolitionists would stop at nothing to destroy their property and civilization (Documents 14 and 15).

Northerners largely took a different view. Republicans, looking ahead to the upcoming election of 1860, took great pains to distance themselves from Brown's violence and vigilantism, while downplaying the rampant conspiracy theories about marauding abolitionists sweeping the South. "Our own belief is that he should not be executed," wrote the editors of the Albany, New York, *Evening Journal*, a paper closely identified with the Republican presidential hopeful William H. Seward (Document 12). "But if the seeds of future excitement are planted on his tomb, we do not doubt it will be found that they were placed there as well by his Southern enemies as by his Northern sympathizers." Northern Democratic papers were far more critical of Brown's actions and motives, and they used the raid as an opportunity to score their own political points. "We do not intend to charge all the members of the black republican party as being responsible for this deplorable affair at Harpers Ferry," wrote the editors of the Concord *New Hampshire Patriot*. "But we ask them to consider whether . . . it is not at least the probable effect . . . of the doctrine of 'irrepressible conflict' which they are now urged to make the sum and substance of their political faith."

On the other side of the Northern political spectrum, abolitionists were busy turning Brown into the most prominent antislavery martyr since Elijah Lovejoy, the newspaper editor whose murder two decades earlier inspired Brown's oath in the Hudson, Ohio, church. Northern intellectuals were especially intent on painting a picture of Brown as a selfless hero (Figure 3). Ralph Waldo Emerson, far and away the leading intellectual of his day, wrote as Brown was awaiting execution that he was "the rarest of heroes, a pure idealist, with no by-ends of his own." Days earlier, Emerson went even further, calling Brown "that new saint than whom nothing purer or more brave was ever led by love of men into conflict and death,—the new saint awaiting his martyrdom, and who, if he shall suffer [execution], will make the gallows glorious like a cross."[40] Another acquaintance of Brown's, the poet Julia Ward Howe, voiced similar sentiments: "[Brown's] attempt [at Harpers Ferry] I must judge insane but the spirit heroic. I should be glad to be as sure of heaven as that old man may be, following right in the spirit and footsteps of the old martyrs, girding on his sword for the weak and oppressed." Howe, of course, later wrote "The Battle Hymn of the Republic," which was set to a familiar tune during the Civil War: "John Brown's Body." Brown's most impassioned defender, however, was the Transcendentalist Henry David Thoreau. In a powerful speech and widely circulated essay (Document 13), Thoreau held up the imprisoned abolitionist as a person to emulate and his accusers as ignorant brutes. "Read his admirable answers to [Governor] Mason and others," Thoreau said after Brown's interrogation was printed in the local press. "How they are dwarfed and defeated by the contrast! On the one side, half-brutish, half-timid questioning; on the other, truth, clear as lightning, crashing into their obscene temples. . . . They are but helpless tools in this great work. It was no human power that gathered them about this preacher."[41]

Despite the escalating rhetoric from the political extremes in both sections, the American public largely allowed the immediate sense of crisis that followed the raid to subside. A fire-eater convention calling for secession held in January 1860, for example, fizzled as most Americans held out the hope that slavery could be safeguarded without destroying the Union. But Brown, his raid, his death, and his prophecy (and the very different interpretation of them by people in both the North and the South) remained just below the surface. Both sides were more than ready to resuscitate the rhetoric and calls for action when the crisis of the Union reached its next boiling point with the election of Abraham Lincoln to the presidency in 1860 without a single Southern electoral vote. Thus, Brown became a symbol in the South as well as the North, for pro- as well as antislavery forces. Ideologues on opposite sides ensured that Brown's final prophecy—that the slavery issue would never be decided without violence and bloodshed— would be borne out.

President Lincoln supposedly greeted Harriet Beecher Stowe, the author of *Uncle Tom's Cabin*, by saying, "So, this is the little lady who

Figure 3. *Imagining John Brown's Last Moments, 1863*

Popular illustrations such as this lithograph published by the famed illustrators Currier & Ives in 1863 helped to burnish Brown's image. Eyewitnesses to Brown's execution did not mention the scene, but it was included in contemporary poems by John Greenleaf Whittier and the Brown biography written by James Redpath. In 1881 the painter Thomas Hovenden created another iconic image of Brown kissing an African American child on the way to the gallows.

The Granger Collection, New York.

wrote the big book that made this great war." Surely the vivid scenes, artful pathos, and memorable sentiment in Stowe's book helped to radicalize Northern opinion and escalate tensions between North and South. But John Brown's brand of intransigence and righteous bloodletting in Kansas and, later, at Harpers Ferry, played a similar role in the Civil War's making as well. It was only fitting that thousands marched into battle during that singularly violent war singing about "John Brown's Body" (Document 16).

NOTES

[1] *U.S. Senate Committee Reports*, 1859–1860, II., 98; James Elliot Cabot, *A Memoir of Ralph Waldo Emerson*, 2 vols. (Boston and New York: Houghton Mifflin), 597.

[2] *New York Herald*, December 21, 1859.

[3] John Brown to Henry L. Stearns, July 15, 1857.

[4] Franklin B. Sanborn, *Life and Letters of John Brown* (Concord, Mass.: Roberts Brothers, 1885), 91–93; Oswald Garrison Villard, *John Brown: A Biography Fifty Years After* (Boston: Houghton Mifflin, 1910), 20.

[5] *The Liberator*, January 1, 1831.

[6] Stephen B. Oates, *To Purge This Land with Blood: A Biography of John Brown* (New York: Harper & Row, 1970), 30–31.

[7] John Brown to Frederick Brown, November 21, 1834, in Sanborn, *Life and Letters of John Brown*, 40–41.

[8] Louis Ruchames, ed., *A John Brown Reader* (London and New York: Abelard-Schuman, 1959), 179–81; Oates, 41–42.

[9] Philip S. Foner, *Life and Writings of Frederick Douglass* (4 vols., New York: New York International Publishers, 1955), II, 49–50.

[10] Sanborn, *Life and Letters of John Brown*, 128–31.

[11] Richard Henry Dana Jr., "How We Met John Brown," *Atlantic Monthly*, 28 (July 1871), 6–7; Oates, *To Purge This Land with Blood*, 68–69.

[12] Sanborn, *Life and Times of John Brown*, 96–97.

[13] Ruchames, *A John Brown Reader*, 76–78.

[14] Chief among these controversies were the Missouri Crisis (1819–1821), Texas annexation (1835–1845), the Mexican War (1846–1848), and the Compromise of 1850.

[15] *Congressional Globe*, 33 Cong., 1 sess., Appendix, 769 (May 25, 1854).

[16] John Brown to John Brown Jr., August 21, 1854.

[17] John Brown Jr. to John Brown, May 20, 24, 1855.

[18] John Brown to Mary Brown, October 13, 1855, in Sanborn, *Life and Times of John Brown*, 200–201.

[19] While there was no loss of life in the famous "sack of Lawrence," free staters and their allies in the East (especially the Republican party press) were successful in casting the event as a ferocious attack against innocent townspeople.

[20] On the complex chronology of events in May 1856, see Salmon Brown, "John Brown and Sons in Kansas Territory," *Indiana Magazine of History* XXXI (June 1935), 142–50. See also Villard, *John Brown*, 151–52; Oates, *To Purge This Land with Blood*, 128–30.

[21] Testimony from Salmon Brown and his son-in-law Henry Thompson (as well as from the murdered men's wives) leaves little doubt that John Brown was involved, even

if he did not himself participate in the slaying. See Villard, *John Brown*, 148–51; Oates, *To Purge This Land with Blood*, 133–37.

[22]James Hanway Collection, #372, Manuscript Volume, 1856, Kansas State Historical Association, 6–7.

[23]James Redpath, *Public Life of Capt. John Brown* (Boston: Thayer and Eldridge, 1860), 112–14.

[24]Even though Osawatomie was burned by border ruffians during the battle, Brown's band of thirty-five men stayed hidden in the brush adjacent to the Osage River and rained bullets down on the invaders.

[25]Villard, *John Brown*, 248.

[26]John H. Kagi, "Journal of the Chatham Convention," 48; Osborn P. Anderson, *A Voice from Harper's Ferry* (Boston: Printed for the author, 1861), 8–9.

[27]Sanborn, *The Life and Times of John Brown*, 438.

[28]Testimony of Richard Realf before the Mason Committee, *U.S. Senate Committee Reports*, 1859–1860, II., 96–99.

[29]Kagi, "Journal," 45–47; Anderson, *A Voice from Harper's Ferry*, 9.

[30]Frederick Douglass, *Life and Times of Frederick Douglass* (Boston: De Wolfe & Fiske Co., 1881; rev. 1892), 322–25.

[31]The interview was first published in the *New York Herald*, October 21, 1859, and reprinted with slight alterations in Sanborn, 562–69.

[32]John Anthony Scott and Robert Scott, *John Brown of Harper's Ferry* (New York: Facts on File, 1988), 153.

[33]David Reynolds, *John Brown: Abolitionist* (New York: Alfred A. Knopf, 2005), 8.

[34]Many newspapers covered the trial. This account is from the *New York Times*, October 27–November 3, 1859. See also Villard, 476–507; Oates, 320–29.

[35]*New York Times*, November 3, 1859; Villard, 498–99.

[36]John Brown to "E.B. of R.I.," November 1, 1859, printed in *The John Brown Invasion*, 47–48; also quoted in Sanborn, 583.

[37]Col. William Fellows, New York *Sun*, February 13, 1898, quoted in Villard, 538–99; *New York Evening Post*, October 23, 1909.

[38]E. E. Peticolas to Henry A. Wise, November 1, 1859, and Dr. Lewis A. Sayre to Henry A. Wise, Tatham Collection, MHS, reprinted in Villard, 504.

[39]Note reproduced in Villard between pp. 554–55. Emphasis in original.

[40]Cabot, *A Memoir of Ralph Waldo Emerson*, 597. The *New York Tribune*'s reporter published the quotation "as glorious as the cross"; the wording gained even more national attention when it was printed in *The Liberator*, November 11, 1859. See John J. McDonald, "Emerson and John Brown," *New England Quarterly*, 44:3 (September 1971), 377–96.

[41]The Transcendentalists' initial forays into Brown hagiography led to a procession of reverential biographies. The Scottish-born newspaperman James Redpath, who covered Brown's Kansas exploits, busied himself in an exercise of heroic mythmaking even before Brown hung from the gallows. The hero of *The Public Life of John Brown* was a "Puritan warrior of the Lord," a saintly "predestined leader of the second and holier American Revolution." Brown's greatest apologist, however, was "Secret Six" member Franklin Sanborn. Sanborn went to his grave denying Brown's part in the Pottawatomie massacre and always sent a significant part of the proceeds from his *Life and Letters of John Brown* (1885) to Brown's widow and surviving family.

The first truly evenhanded biography was not published until the fiftieth anniversary of John Brown's raid. Its author, Oswald Garrison Villard, was the grandson of the abolitionist William Lloyd Garrison and one of the founders of the National Association for the Advancement of Colored People (NAACP). With his bloodlines and penchant for social activism, many observers predicted Villard's *John Brown: A Biography Fifty Years After* would be his generation's heir to Redpath and Sanborn. In this they were mistaken. Villard's Brown was a mélange of unpleasant contradictions: a bumbling, violent misanthrope who somehow coexisted as a Christian fanatic and a bloodthirsty killer. Ironically it was only during his last—and most dramatic—failure that Brown stumbled onto anything remotely approaching greatness. John Brown was an icon of liberty but only by a kind of fanatical accident. Apparently Villard's portrayal was not bloodthirsty enough for Hill Peebles Wilson, who published the all-but-unreadable *John Brown, Soldier of Fortune: A Critique* in 1913 to "correct" Villard's lenient portrait.

Since Villard's biography appeared, historians have expended considerable effort trying to identify the "real" John Brown. W. E. B. Du Bois's *John Brown* portrays its hero as a crusader for right against wrong. David Karsner attempted to balance both sides in *John Brown: Terrible Saint*, published in 1934. For James G. Malin, a historian at the University of Kansas and author of *John Brown and the Legend of Fifty-Six* (1942), Brown was the worst kind of hypocrite. Benjamin Quarles wrote numerous laudatory books about John Brown's special relationship with African Americans, including *Allies for Freedom: Blacks and John Brown* (1934). Brown's ablest biographer, Stephen Oates, published his sympathetic portrait *To Purge This Land with Blood* in 1970, as the civil rights movement was cresting. The literary scholar David Reynolds's recent biography of Brown, *John Brown, Abolitionist*, portrays him as an "American terrorist," driven by religious certainty—but one who murdered only for the noble goal of creating a democratic society. Even the talented novelist Russell Banks tried to get at the inner John Brown with his magisterial novel *Cloudsplitter* (1999), which tells the story of Brown's life through the eyes of his son Owen, one of the survivors of Harpers Ferry. Even in the hands of a novelist who can invent relationships and conversations, John Brown's brain remains tough to crack. Was he good or evil? A Hebrew warrior-prophet or Cromwellian Roundhead? Martyr or lunatic? Perhaps by getting back to the original documents, this book can help its readers get closer to the answers of these befuddling questions.

The Harpers Ferry Raid: Dramatis Personae

The Raiders

Killed during the Raid, October 17–19, 1859:
  Anderson, Jeremiah
  Brown, Oliver
  Brown, Watson
  Kagi, John Henry
  Leary, Lewis
  Leeman, William H.
  Newby, Dangerfield
  Thompson, Dauphin
  Thompson, William
  Taylor, Stewart

Executed by the State of Virginia:
  Brown, John (December 2, 1859)
  Cook, John E. (December 16, 1859)
  Copeland, John A. (December 16, 1859)
  Coppoc, Edwin (December 16, 1859)
  Green, Shields (December 16, 1859)
  Hazlett, Albert (March 16, 1860)
  Stevens, Aaron D. (March 16, 1860)

Survived the Raid:
  Anderson, Osborne P.
  Brown, Owen
  Coppoc, Barclay
  Merriam, Francis Jackson
  Tidd, Charles Plummer

Militia and U.S. Marines

Brevet Colonel Robert E. Lee
Lieutenant J. E. B. Stewart
Colonel Lewis Washington

Elected Officials

Representative Charles Faulkner (Virginia)
Senator James Mason (Virginia)
Representative Clement Vallandigham (Ohio)
Governor Henry Wise (Virginia)

PART TWO

The Documents

1

The Making of a Radical Abolitionist

1

JOHN BROWN

Words of Advice to the United States League of Gileadites

January 15, 1851

As a result of victory in the war with Mexico (1846–1848), the United States gained undisputed control of Texas and territory that was to become California, Nevada, and Utah and parts of Colorado, Arizona, New Mexico, and Wyoming. Whether these vast new lands would remain free (as they had been under Mexican law) or be open to slavery became a major political issue. Two years after the war ended, Congress passed the Compromise of 1850 in an attempt to end the political standoff. (See Map 1, page 14.) Gold-rich California entered the Union as a free state, and the slave trade was banned in the District of Columbia, but slaveholders were the big winners under the Compromise. In addition to the possibility that New Mexico would be open to slavery, the South received the tough federal Fugitive Slave Law its representatives had long demanded. Virginia Senator James Mason, who would later interview John Brown at Harpers Ferry and lead a Senate panel on the raid, wrote the law.

Northern antislavery groups were outraged. The law required citizens to aid in the recovery of runaways, imposed penalties on marshals who refused to enforce the law or from whom an ex-slave should escape, and denied a fugitive's right to a jury trial. Cases were to be handled by special commissioners, who would be paid $5 if the alleged fugitive was released

Franklin Sanborn, *Life and Letters of John Brown* (London: Sampson Low, Marson, Searle, & Irvington, 1885), 124–27.

and $10 if he or she was returned to bondage. For John Brown, the passage of the Fugitive Slave Law was further evidence that bold action was needed to resist slavery's encroachments. With inspiration from the Book of Judges in the Hebrew Bible, Brown wrote his "Words of Advice" and presented them to the free blacks of Springfield. The only way to defeat the slaveholders who controlled the U.S. government, he said, was to form guerilla bands and fight. "Stand by one another and by your friends, while a drop of blood remains," he told the new group. "Be hanged, if you must, but tell no tales out of school. Make no confession."

Forty-four black women and men agreed to join Brown's United States League of Gileadites. The "Words of Advice" clearly reflect militant black abolitionists' influence on Brown.

"Union Is Strength"

Nothing so charms the American people as personal bravery. Witness the case of Cinques,[1] of everlasting memory, on board the "Amistad." The trial for life of one bold and to some extent successful man, for defending his rights in good earnest, would arouse more sympathy throughout the nation than the accumulated wrongs and sufferings of more than three millions of our submissive colored population. We need not mention the Greeks struggling against the oppressive Turks, the Poles against Russia, nor the Hungarians against Austria and Russia combined, to prove this. *No jury can be found in the Northern States that would convict a man for defending his rights to the last extremity. This is well understood by Southern Congressmen, who insisted that the right of trial by jury should not be granted to the fugitive.* Colored people have ten times the number of fast friends among the whites than they suppose, and would have ten times the number they now have were they but half as much in earnest to secure their dearest rights as they are to ape the follies and extravagances of their white neighbors, and to indulge in idle show, in ease, and in luxury. Just think of the money expended by individuals in your behalf in the past twenty years! Think of the number who have been mobbed and imprisoned on your account! Have any of you seen the Branded Hand? Do you remember the names of Lovejoy and Torrey?[2]

---

[1]A West African man, born Sengbe Pieh, who was the most prominent defendant in the *Amistad* slave case. His Spanish captors referred to him as "Cinque."

[2]Elijah Lovejoy (1802–1837) and Charles Torrey (1813–1846) were white abolitionists who died working to abolish slavery in the United States.

Should one of your number be arrested, you must collect together as quickly as possible, so as to outnumber your adversaries who are taking an active part against you. Let no able-bodied man appear on the ground unequipped, or with his weapons exposed to view: let that be understood beforehand. Your plans must be known only to yourself, and with the understanding that all traitors must die, wherever caught and proven to be guilty. "Whosoever is fearful or afraid, let him return and part early from Mount Gilead" (Judges, vii. 3; Deut. xx. 8). Give all cowards an opportunity to show it on condition of holding their peace. *Do not delay one moment after you are ready: you will lose all your resolution if you do. Let the first blow be the signal for all to engage; and when engaged do not do your work by halves, but make clean work with your enemies, — and be sure you meddle not with any others.* By going about your business quietly, you will get the job disposed of before the number that an uproar would bring together can collect; and you will have the advantage of those who come out against you, for they will be wholly unprepared with either equipments or matured plans; all with them will be confusion and terror. Your enemies will be slow to attack you after you have done up the work nicely; and if they should, they will have to encounter your white friends as well as you; for you may safely calculate on a division of the whites, and may by that means get to an honorable parley.

Be firm, determined, and cool; but let it be understood that you are not to be driven to desperation without making it an awful dear job to others as well as to you. Give them to know distinctly that those who live in wooden houses should not throw fire, and that you are just as able to suffer as your white neighbors. *After effecting a rescue, if you are assailed, go into the houses of your most prominent and influential white friends with your wives; and that will effectually fasten upon them the suspicion of being connected with you, and will compel them to make a common cause with you, whether they would otherwise live up to their profession or not. This would leave them no choice in the matter.* Some would doubtless prove themselves true of their own choice; others would flinch. That would be taking them at their own words. You may make a tumult in the court-room where a trial is going on, by burning gunpowder freely in paper packages, if you cannot think of any better way to create a momentary alarm, and might possibly give one or more of your enemies a hoist. But in such case the prisoner will need to take the hint at once, and bestir himself; and so should his friends improve the opportunity for a general rush.

A lasso might possibly be applied to a slave-catcher for once with good effect. Hold on to your weapons, and never be persuaded to leave them, part with them, or have them far away from you. *Stand by one another and by your friends, while a drop of blood remains; and be hanged, if you must, but tell no tales out of school. Make no confession.*

Union is strength. Without some well-digested arrangements nothing to any good purpose is likely to be done, let the demand be never so great. Witness the case of Hamlet and Long in New York, when there was no well-defined plan of operations or suitable preparation beforehand.

The desired end may be effectually secured by the means proposed; namely, the enjoyment of our inalienable rights.

Agreement

As citizens of the United States of America, trusting in a just and merciful God, whose spirit and all-powerful aid we humbly implore, *we will ever be true to the flag of our beloved country, always acting under it.* We, whose names are hereunto affixed, do constitute ourselves a branch of the United States League of Gileadites. That we will provide ourselves at once with suitable implements, and will aid those who do not possess the means, if any such are disposed to join us. We invite every colored person whose heart is engaged in the performance of our business, whether male or female, old or young. The duty of the aged, infirm, and young members of the League shall be to give instant notice to all members in case of an attack upon any of our people. We agree to have no officers except a treasurer and secretary *pro tem.,* until after some trial of courage and talent of able-bodied members shall enable us to elect officers from those who shall have rendered the most important services. Nothing but wisdom and undaunted courage, efficiency, and general good conduct shall in any way influence us in electing our officers. . . .

RESOLUTIONS OF THE SPRINGFIELD BRANCH
OF THE UNITED STATES LEAGUE OF GILEADITES.
ADOPTED 15TH JAN., 1851.

1. *Resolved*, That we, whose names are affixed, do constitute ourselves a Branch of the United States League, under the above name.

2. *Resolved*, That all business of this Branch be conducted with the utmost quiet and good order; that we individually provide ourselves with suitable implements without delay; and that we will sufficiently aid those who do not possess the means, if any such are disposed to join us.

3. *Resolved*, That a committee of one or more discreet, influential men be appointed to collect the names of all colored persons whose heart is engaged for the performance of our business, whether male or female, whether old or young.

4. *Resolved*, That the appropriate duty of all aged, infirm, female, or youthful members of this Branch is to give instant notice to all other members of any attack upon the rights of our people, first informing all able-bodied men of this League or Branch, and next, all well known friends of the colored people; and *that this information be confined to such alone,* that there may be as little excitement as possible, and no noise in the so doing.

5. *Resolved*, That a committee of one or more discreet persons be appointed to ascertain the condition of colored persons in regard to implements, and to instruct others in regard to their conduct in any emergency.

6. *Resolved*, That no other officer than a *treasurer*, with a president and secretary *pro tem.*, be appointed by this Branch, until after some trial of the courage and talents of able-bodied members shall enable a majority of the members to elect their officers from those who *shall have rendered the most important services.*

7. *Resolved*, That, trusting in a just and merciful God, whose *spirit* and *all-powerful aid* we humbly implore, we will most cheerfully and heartily support and obey such officers, when chosen as before; and that nothing but *wisdom, undaunted courage, efficiency*, and *general good conduct* shall in any degree influence our individual votes in case of such election.

8. *Resolved*, That a meeting of all members of this Branch shall be immediately called for the purpose of electing officers (to be chosen immediately by ballot) after the first trial *shall have been made* of the qualifications of individual members for such command, as before mentioned.

9. *Resolved*, That as citizens of the United States of America we will ever be found true to the flag of our beloved country, always acting under it.

This is signed by the following members:—

B. C. Dowling.	Henry Johnson.	Henry Hector.
John Smith.	G. W. Holmes.	John Strong.
Reverdy Johnson.	C. A. Gazam.	Wm. Burns.
Samuel Chandler.	Eliza Green.	Wm. Gordon.
J. N. Howard.	Jane Fowler.	Joseph Addams.

Charles Rollins.   H. J. Jones.   Wm. Green.
Scipio Webb.   Ann Johnson.   Wm. H. Montague.
Charles Odell.   Cyrus Thomas.   Jane Wicks.
L. Wallace.   Henry Robinson.   James Madison.
  And seventeen others.

2

KANSAS TERRITORIAL LEGISLATURE

An Act to Punish Offenses against Slave Property

1855

In the wake of the Compromise of 1850, the U.S. government opened the territories of Kansas and Nebraska, parts of the original Louisiana Purchase. (See Map 1.) The Kansas-Nebraska Act, signed into law in May 1854, set off a race between pro- and antislavery settlers to determine whether Kansas would enter the Union as a free or slave state. The first wave of settlers came from nearby Missouri, where slavery was legal. But in the North, abolitionists formed the New England Emigrant Aid Company, which sent settlers to Kansas to secure it as a free territory. By mid-1855, approximately 1,200 Northerners had made the journey to the new territory, including John Brown's sons Owen, Salmon, John Jr., Jason, and Frederick. John Brown did not immediately join his sons, saying he felt "committed to operate in another part of the field."

In an election to choose a territorial legislature in March 1855, almost 5,000 Missourians (called "border ruffians" in the antislavery press) illegally poured over the state line to elect proslavery candidates. Although, Kansas Territory had only 2,905 registered voters, 6,307 ballots were cast, and 87 percent of those favored slavery. The fraudulently elected state legislature enacted laws, including this one, that incorporated and strengthened Missouri's slave code. Severe punishments were mandated for anyone who spoke or wrote against slaveholding, and anyone caught assisting fugitives was sentenced to death or ten years of hard labor. Northerners were outraged, and John Jr. wrote to his father about

Kansas Territory *Statutes* (1855): 715–17. Kansas State Historical Society.

the violence that was sure to come and make Kansas bleed. On May 24, 1855, John Brown wrote his sons that he had changed his mind: He was coming to Kansas to join the fight. Brown's time in Kansas would mark his transition from a failed businessman and frustrated abolitionist organizer to an antislavery warrior who used violence to advance his goals.

SEC. 3. If any free person shall, by speaking, writing, or printing, advise, persuade, or induce any slaves to rebel, conspire against, or murder any citizen of this Territory, or shall bring into, print, write, publish, or circulate, or cause to be brought into, printed, written, published, or circulated, or *shall knowingly aid or assist in the bringing into, printing, writing, publishing, or circulating, in this Territory any book, pamphlet, paper, magazine, or circular, for the purpose of exciting insurrection, rebellion, revolt, or conspiracy on the part of the slaves, free negroes, or mulattoes,* against the citizens of the Territory or any part of them, such person shall be guilty of felony, *and suffer death.*

SEC. 4. If any person shall entice, decoy, or carry away out of this Territory any slave belonging to another, with intent to deprive the owner thereof of the services of such slave, or with intent to effect or procure the freedom of such slave, he shall be adjudged guilty of grand larceny, and on conviction thereof, *shall suffer death,* or be imprisoned at hard labor for not less than ten years.

SEC. 5. If any person shall aid or assist in enticing, decoying, persuading, or carrying away, or sending out of this Territory any slave belonging to another, with intent to effect or procure the freedom of such slave, or with intent to deprive the owner thereof of the services of such slave, he shall be adjudged guilty of grand larceny, and on conviction thereof *he shall suffer death,* or be imprisoned at hard labor for not less than ten years.

SEC. 6. If any person shall entice, decoy, or carry away out of any State or other Territory of the United States any slave belonging to another, with intent to procure or effect the freedom of such slave, or to deprive the owners thereof of the services of such slave, and shall bring such slave into this Territory, he shall be adjudged guilty of grand larceny, in the same manner as if such slave had been enticed, decoyed, or carried away out of this Territory; and in such case the larceny may be charged to have been committed in any county of this Territory into or through which such slave shall have been brought by such person; and on conviction thereof, the person offending *shall suffer death,* or be imprisoned at hard labor for not less than ten years.

. . .

SEC. 9. If any person shall resist any officer while attempting to arrest any slave that may have escaped from the service of his master or owner, or shall rescue such slave when in the custody of any officer or other person, or shall entice, persuade, aid, or assist such slave from the custody of any officer or other person who may have such slave in custody, whether such slave have escaped from the service of his master or owner in this Territory or in any other State or Territory, the person so offending shall be guilty of felony, and punished by imprisonment at hard labor for a term not less than two years.

. . .

SEC. 11. If any person print, write, introduce into, publish, or circulate, or cause to be brought into, printed, written, published, or circulated, or shall knowingly aid or assist in bringing into, printing, publishing, or circulating within this Territory any book, paper, pamphlet, magazine, handbill, or circular containing *any statements, arguments, opinions, sentiment, doctrine, advice, or innuendo calculated to produce a disorderly, dangerous, or rebellious disaffection among the slaves of this Territory, or to induce such slaves to escape from the service of their masters, or resist their authority, he shall be guilty of felony, and be punished by imprisonment at hard labor for a term not less than five years.*

SEC. 12. If any free person, by speaking or by writing, assert or maintain that persons have not the right to hold slaves in this Territory, or shall introduce into this Territory, print, publish, write, circulate, or cause to be printed, published, written, circulated, or introduced into this Territory, any book, paper, magazine, pamphlet, or circular containing any denial of the right of persons to hold slaves in this Territory, such person shall be deemed guilty of felony, and punished by imprisonment at hard labor for a term not less than two years.

SEC. 13. No person who is conscientiously opposed to holding slaves, or who does not admit the right to hold slaves in this Territory, shall sit as a juror on the trial of any prosecution for any violation of any of the sections of this act.

3

JOHN BROWN

Letter to Wife and Children from Kansas Territory

December 16, 1855

Soon after John Brown arrived in Kansas, the tense standoff between pro- and antislavery settlers was becoming violent. After a proslavery settler shot slavery opponent Charles Dow in November 1855, an army of Missourians under the command of the proslavery sheriff Samuel Jones crossed the state line to lay siege on the "free state" town of Lawrence. Brown, longing for an opportunity to strike out with force against slavery and slaveholders, loaded a wagon with provisions and weapons and set out for Lawrence. When Brown and his party reached the encampment, guns and knives drawn, stunned Missourians let them pass unharmed. In town, Brown was quickly commissioned as a captain in the First Brigade of Kansas Volunteers and given command of a small company of men.

John Brown did not attack anyone in 1855; instead, free-state leaders Charles Robinson and James Lane negotiated a favorable peace treaty with Territorial Governor Wilson Shannon that temporarily diffused the situation. Brown laid out the entire episode in a letter to his family back in New York. John Brown had most certainly arrived in Kansas and assumed his new identity as a man of action and a fighter who would stand up to slaveholders and their allies.

OSAWATOMIE, K. T., DEC. 16, 1855.
Sabbath Evening.

DEAR WIFE AND CHILDREN, EVERY ONE, — I improve the first mail since my return from the camp of volunteers, who lately turned out for the defence of the town of Lawrence in this Territory; and notwithstanding I suppose you have learned the result before this (possibly), will give a brief account of the invasion in my own way.

Franklin Sanborn, *Life and Letters of John Brown* (London: Sampson Low, Marson, Searle, & Irvington, 1885), 217–21.

About three or four weeks ago news came that a Free-State man by the name of Dow had been murdered by a proslavery man by the name of Coleman, who had gone and given himself up for trial to the proslavery Governor Shannon. This was soon followed by further news that a Free-State man who was the only reliable witness against the murderer had been seized by a Missourian (appointed sheriff by the bogus Legislature of Kansas) upon false pretexts, examined, and held to bail under such heavy bonds, to answer to those false charges, as he could not give; that while on his way to trial, in charge of the bogus sheriff, he was rescued by some men belonging to a company near Lawrence; and that in consequence of the rescue Governor Shannon had ordered out all the proslavery force he could muster in the Territory, and called on Missouri for further help; that about two thousand had collected, demanding a surrender of the rescued witness and of the rescuers, the destruction of several buildings and printing-presses, and a giving up of the Sharpe's rifles by the Free-State men,—threatening to destroy the town with cannon, with which they were provided, etc.; that about an equal number of Free-State men had turned out to resist them, and that a battle was hourly expected or supposed to have been already fought.

These reports appeared to be well authenticated, but we could get no further account of matters; and I left this for the place where the boys are settled, at evening, intending to go to Lawrence to learn the facts the next day. John was, however, started on horseback; but before he had gone many rods, word came that our help was immediately wanted. On getting this last news, it was at once agreed to break up at John's camp, and take Wealthy and Johnny to Jason's camp (some two miles off), and that all the men but Henry, Jason, and Oliver should at once set off for Lawrence under arms; those three being wholly unfit for duty. We then set about providing a little corn-bread and meat, blankets, and cooking utensils, running bullets and loading all our guns, pistols, etc. The five set off in the afternoon, and after a short rest in the night (which was quite dark), continued our march until after daylight next morning, when we got our breakfast, started again, and reached Lawrence in the forenoon, all of us more or less lamed by our tramp. On reaching the place we found that negotiations had commenced between Governor Shannon (having a force of some fifteen or sixteen hundred men) and the principal leaders of the Free-State men, they having a force of some five hundred men at that time. These were busy, night and day, fortifying the town with embankments and circular earthworks, up to the time of the treaty with the Governor, as an attack was constantly looked for, notwithstanding the negotiations then pending. This state of things continued from Friday until Sunday evening. On the evening we left Osawatomie a company of the invaders, of from fifteen to twenty-five, attacked some three or four Free-State men, mostly unarmed, killing a Mr. Barber from Ohio, wholly unarmed. His body was afterward brought in and lay for some days in the room afterward occupied by a part of the company to which we belong (it being organized after we reached Lawrence). The building was a large unfinished stone hotel, in which a great part of the volunteers were quartered, who witnessed the scene of bringing in the wife and other friends of the murdered man. I will only say of this scene that it was heart-rending, and calculated to exasperate the men exceedingly, and one of the sure results of civil war.

After frequently calling on the leaders of the Free-State men to come and have an interview with him, by Governor Shannon, and after as often getting for an answer that if he had any business to transact with any one in Lawrence, to come and attend to it, he signified his wish to come into the town, and an escort was sent to the invaders' camp to conduct him in. When there, the leading Free-State men, finding out his weakness, frailty, and consciousness of the awkward circumstances into which he had really got himself, took advantage of his cowardice and folly, and by means of that and the free use of whiskey and some trickery succeeded in getting a written arrangement with him much to their own liking. He stipulated with them to order the proslavery men of Kansas home, and to proclaim to the Missouri invaders that they must quit the Territory without delay, and also to give up General Pomeroy (a prisoner in their camp),—which was all done; he also recognizing the volunteers as the militia of Kansas, and empowering their officers to call them out whenever in their discretion the safety of Lawrence or other portions of the Territory might require it to be done. He (Governor Shannon) gave up all pretension of further attempt to enforce the enactments of the bogus Legislature, and retired, subject to the derision and scoffs of the Free-State men (into whose hands he had committed the welfare and protection of Kansas), and to the pity of some and the curses of others of the invading force.

So ended this last Kansas invasion,—the Missourians returning with *flying colors*, after incurring heavy expenses, suffering great exposure, hardships, and privations, not having fought any battles, burned or destroyed any infant towns or Abolition presses; leaving the Free-State men organized and armed, and in full possession of the Territory; not having fulfilled any of all their dreadful threatenings, except to murder one *unarmed* man, and to commit some robberies and waste of property upon defenceless families, unfortunately within their power. We learn by their papers that they boast of a great victory over the Abolitionists; and well they may. Free-State men have only hereafter to retain the footing they have gained, and *Kansas is free.* Yesterday the people passed upon the Free-State constitution. The result, though not yet known, no one doubts.

One little circumstance, connected with our own number, showing a little of the true character of those invaders: On our way, about three miles from Lawrence, we had to pass a bridge (with our arms and ammunition) of which the invaders held possession; but as the five of us had each a gun, with two large revolvers in a belt exposed to view, with a third in his pocket, and as we moved directly on to the bridge without making any halt, they for some reason suffered us to pass without interruption, notwithstanding there were some fifteen to twenty-five (as variously reported) stationed in a log-house at one end of the bridge. We could not count them. A boy on our approach ran and gave them notice. Five others of our company, well armed, who followed us some miles behind, met with equally civil treatment the same day. After we left to go to Lawrence, until we returned when disbanded, I did not see the least sign of cowardice or want of self-possession exhibited by any volunteer of the eleven companies who constituted the Free-State force; and I never expect again to see an equal number of such well-behaved, cool, determined men,—fully, as I believe, sustaining the high character of the Revolutionary fathers. But enough of this, as we intend to send you a paper giving a more full account of the affair. We have cause for gratitude in that we all returned safe and well, with the exception of hard colds, and found those left behind rather improving.

We have received fifty dollars from father, and learn from him that he has sent you the same amount,—for which we ought to be grateful, as we are much relieved, both as respects ourselves and you. The mails have been kept back during the invasion, but we hope to hear from you again soon. Mr. Adair's folks are well, or nearly so. Weather mostly pleasant, but sometimes quite severe. No snow of account as yet. Can think of but little more to-night.

Monday Morning, December 17.

The ground for the first time is barely whitened with snow, and it is quite cold; but we have before had a good deal of cold weather, with heavy rains. Henry and Oliver and, I may [say], Jason were disappointed in not being able to go to war. The disposition at both our camps to turn out was uniform. I believe I have before acknowledged the receipt of a letter from you and Watson. Have just taken one from the office for Henry that I think to be from Ruth. Do write often, and let me know all about how you get along through the winter. May God abundantly bless you all, and make you faithful.

Your affectionate husband and father,

JOHN BROWN

4

MAHALA DOYLE AND
LOUISA JANE WILKINSON

Accounts of the Pottawatomie Massacre

1856

Throughout the winter of 1855–1856, rumors of an imminent proslavery "invasion" spread rapidly through the antislavery settlements in Kansas. The rumors proved false until May 21, 1856, when an army of Missourians — led by the proslavery U.S. Senator David Rice Atchison — sacked the town of Lawrence and burned down the Free-State Hotel. The Browns and their Osawatomie allies quickly assembled to aid the people of Lawrence. Already furious that the abolitionist defenders of the town refused to fight back, Brown pledged action. He might have already learned that Massachusetts Senator Charles Sumner had been beaten nearly to death by a South Carolina congressman after delivering a speech called "The Crime against Kansas."

After dark on May 24, 1856, Brown, his sons, his son-in-law Henry Thompson, and two others arrived at James Doyle's house on nearby Pottawatomie Creek. Announcing themselves as the "Northern army," the group forced three of the Doyle men out of hiding and attacked them with broadswords. Proceeding down the creek, Brown's party killed Allen Wilkinson and then William Sherman. None of these men owned slaves,

---

U.S. House Committee Reports, 1855–1856, II, 105–6.

although some were members of the proslavery Law and Order party. Whether John Brown himself participated in the killings has long been a matter of dispute, much of it caused by Brown's refusal to confess formally. But he was clearly the leader of the expedition and decided who would die and who would be spared. The sack of Lawrence and the Pottawatomie killings unleashed a civil war known as Bleeding Kansas in the territory; it ended only after fifty-five people had been killed and the U.S. Army was called in to enforce a cease-fire.

The following accounts of these events are taken from the Congressional Howard Committee Report. The first is from Mahala Doyle, James Doyle's widow, and the second is from Louisa Jane Wilkinson, Allen Wilkinson's widow.

Testimony of Mrs. Doyle

I am the widow of the late James P. Doyle. We moved into the Territory—that is, my husband, myself, and children—moved into the Territory of Kansas some time in November, A.D. 1855, and settled upon Musketo creek, about one mile from its mouth, and where it empties into Pottawatomie creek, in Franklin county. On Saturday, the 24th of May, A.D. 1855, about eleven o'clock at night, after we had all retired, my husband, James P. Doyle, myself, and six children, five boys and one girl—the eldest is about twenty-two years of age; his name is William. The next is about twenty years of age; his name is Drury. The next is about seventeen years of age; his name is John. The next is about thirteen years of age; her name is Polly Ann. The next is about eight years of age; his name is James. The next is about five years of age; his name is Henry. We were all in bed, when we heard some persons come into the yard, and rap at the door, and call for Mr. Doyle, my husband. This was about eleven o'clock on Saturday night, of the 24th of May last. My husband got up and went to the door. Those outside inquired for Mr. Wilkinson, and where he lived. My husband said he would tell them. Mr. Doyle, my husband, and several [men] came into the house, and said they were from the army. My husband was a pro-slavery man. They told my husband that he and the boys must surrender; they were then prisoners. The men were armed with pistols and large knives. They first took my husband out of the house; then took two of my sons—William and Drury—out, and then took my husband and these two boys (William and Drury) away. My son John was spared, because I asked them, in tears, to spare him.

In a short time afterwards I heard the report of pistols; I heard two reports. After which I heard moaning as if a person was dying. Then I heard a wild whoop. They had asked before they went away for our horses. We told them that our horses were out on the prairie. My husband and two boys, my sons, did not come back any more. I went out next morning in search of them, and found my husband and William, my son, lying dead in the road, near together, about two hundred yards from the house. They were buried the next day. On the day of the burying, I saw the dead body of Drury. Fear [for] myself and the remaining children induced me to leave the home where we had been living. We had improved our claim a little. I left and went to the State of Missouri.

Testimony of Mrs. Wilkinson

... On the 25th of May last, somewhere between the hours of midnight and daybreak, I cannot say exactly at what hour, after we all had retired to bed, we were disturbed by the barking of the dog. I was sick with the measles, and woke up Mr. Wilkinson, and asked him if he heard the noise, and what it meant. He said it was only some one passing about, and soon after was again asleep. It was not long before the dog raged and barked furiously, awakening me once more; pretty soon I heard footsteps as of men approaching; saw one pass by the window, and some one knocked at the door. I asked, "Who is that?" No one answered. I awoke my husband, who asked, "Who is that?" Some one replied, "I want you to tell me the way to Dutch Henry's." He commenced to tell them, and they said, "Come out and show us." He wanted to go, but I would not let him; he then told them it was difficult to find his clothes, and could tell them as well without going out of doors. The men out of doors after that stepped back, and I thought I could hear them whispering; but they immediately returned, and as they approached, one of them asked my husband, "Are you a Northern armist?" He answered, "I am." I understood the answer to mean that my husband was opposed to the Northern or Free-Soil party. I cannot say that I understood the question. My husband was a pro-slavery man, and was a member of the Territorial Legislature held at Shawnee Mission. When my husband said, "I am," one of them said, "You are my prisoner; do you surrender?" He said, "Gentlemen, I do." They said, "Open the door." Mr. Wilkinson told them to wait till he made a light, and they replied, "If you don't open it, we will open it for you." He opened the door against my wishes; four men came in; my husband was told to put on his clothes, and they asked him if there were not more men about. They searched for arms, and took a gun and powder-flask,—all the weapon that was about the house. I begged them to let Mr. Wilkinson stay with me, saying that I was sick and helpless, and could not stay by myself. The old man, who seemed to be in command, looked at me, and then around at the children, and replied, "You have neighbors." I said, "So I have; but they are not here, and I cannot go for them." The old man replied, "It matters not." They then took my husband away. One of them came back and took two saddles; I asked what they were going to do with him, and he said, "Take him a prisoner to the camp." I wanted one of them to stay with me. He said "he would, but they would not let him." After they were gone, I thought I heard my husband's voice in complaint, but do not know; [I] went to the door, and all was still. Next morning Mr. Wilkinson was found about one hundred and fifty yards from the house, in some dead brush. I believe that one of Captain Brown's sons was in the party who murdered my husband; I heard a voice like his. I do not know Captain Brown himself. The old man who seemed to be commander wore soiled clothes and a straw hat, pulled down over his face. He spoke quick; [he] is a tall, narrow-faced, elderly man. I would recognize him if I could see him. My husband was a quiet man, and was not engaged in arresting or disturbing anybody.

5

JOHN BROWN

An Idea of Things in Kansas
1857

John Brown's exploits in Kansas were covered by dozens of newspaper correspondents, and as a result his fame grew substantially. Brown, a wanted man after the Pottawatomie killings, provided colorful stories for readers back East. His growing reputation as an abolitionist warrior received additional coverage after the battles of Black Jack (where Brown took a much larger proslavery company prisoner in June 1856)

Franklin Sanborn, *Life and Letters of John Brown* (London: Sampson Low, Marson, Searle, & Irvington, 1885), 243–46.

and Osawatomie (where Brown and his massively outnumbered band were forced to watch their enemies burn a free-state town to the ground on August 30).

Brown traveled to New England in January 1857 to raise funds and arms for continued action in Kansas. He was greeted as a celebrity by some of the region's leading philanthropists, abolitionists, and business-men. During this fundraising trip, Brown met most of the men who helped finance his plans for the Harpers Ferry raid and came to be known as the Secret Six: Franklin Sanborn, George L. Stearns, Thomas Wentworth Higginson, Dr. Samuel Gridley Howe, the Reverend Theodore Parker, and Gerrit Smith. Brown also made public appeals for money and guns in New England towns and cities like Hartford, Boston, and Concord. Brown made notes for these speeches, now housed in the Kansas State Historical Society, in which he outlined the various crimes committed by Missourians and the corrupt territorial government in Kansas. Signifi-cantly, he also cast himself as the main protagonist in the struggle to make Kansas free, detailing his personal sufferings, the death of his son Frederick in battle, and how U.S. troops had ignominiously marched his other sons in chains from Osawatomie to Tecumseh. He even produced a heavy, clanking chain as a prop, claiming the torture rendered his sane son "a maniac—yes, a maniac." Brown knew his audience well, return-ing time and again to the monetary losses and property damage endured by the brave pioneers of Kansas. During the trip, he expertly played the part of the gritty and upstanding freedom fighter.

I propose, in order to make this meeting as useful and interesting as I can, to try and give a correct idea of the condition of things in Kansas, as they were while I was there, and as I suppose they still are, so far as the great question at issue is concerned. And here let me remark that in Kansas the question is never raised of a man, Is he a Demo-crat? Is he a Republican? The questions there raised are, Is he a Free-State man? or, Is he a proslavery man?

I saw, while in Missouri in the fall of 1855, large numbers on their way to Kansas to vote, and also returning after they had so done, as they said. I, together with four of my sons, was called out to help defend Lawrence in the fall of 1855, and travelled most of the way on foot, and during a dark night, a distance of thirty-five miles, where we were detained with some five hundred others, or thereabout, from five to fifteen days,—say an average of ten days,—at a cost to each per day of $1.50 as wages, to say nothing of the actual loss and suffering it occasioned; many of them leaving their families at home sick, their crops not secured, their houses unprepared for winter, and many of them without houses at all. This was the case with myself and all my sons, who were unable to get any house built after our return. The loss in that case, as wages alone, would amount to $7,500. Loss and suffering in consequence cannot be estimated. I saw at that time the body of the murdered Barber, and was present when his wife and other friends were brought in to see him as he lay in the clothes he had on when killed,—no very pleasant sight!

I went, in the spring of last year, with some of my sons among the Buford men, in the character of a surveyor, to see and hear from them their business into the Territory; this took us from our work. I and numerous others, in the spring of last year, travelled some ten miles or over on foot, to meet and advise as to what should be done to meet the gathering storm; this occasioned much loss of time. I also, with many others, about the same time travelled on foot a similar distance to attend a meeting of Judge Cato's court, to find out what kind of laws he intended to enforce; this occasioned further loss of time. I with six sons and a son-in-law was again called out to defend Lawrence, May 20 and 21, and travelled most of the way on foot and during the night, being thirty-five miles. From that date none of us could do any work about our homes, but lost our whole time until we left, in October last, excepting one of my sons, who had a few weeks to devote to the care of his own and his brother's family, who had been burned out of their houses while the two men were prisoners.

From about the 20th of May of last year hundreds of men like ourselves lost their whole time, and entirely failed of securing any kind of crop whatever. I believe it safe to say that five hundred Free-State men lost each one hundred and twenty days, at $1.50 per day, which would be, to say nothing of attendant losses, $90,000. I saw the ruins of many Free-State men's houses at different places in the Territory, together with stacks of grain wasted and burning, to the amount of, say $50,000; making, in lost time and destruction of property, more than $150,000. On or about the 30th of May last two of my sons, with several others, were imprisoned without other crime than opposition to bogus enactments, and most barbarously treated for a time,—one being held about one month, the other about four months. Both had their families in Kansas, and destitute of homes, being burned out after they were imprisoned. In this burning all the eight were sufferers, as we all had our effects at the two houses. One of my sons had his oxen taken from him at this time, and never recovered them. Here is the chain with which one of them was confined, after the cruelty, sufferings, and anxiety he underwent had rendered him a maniac,— yes, a maniac.

On the 2d of June last my son-in-law was terribly wounded (supposed to be mortally), and two other Free-State men, at Black Jack. On the 6th or 7th of June last one of my sons was wounded by accident in camp (supposed to be mortally), and may prove a cripple for life. In August last I was present and saw the mangled and shockingly disfigured body of the murdered Hoyt, of Deerfield, Mass., brought into our camp. I knew him well. I saw several other Free-State men who were either killed or wounded, whose names I cannot now remember. I saw Dr. Graham, who was a prisoner with the ruffians on the 2d of June last, and was present when they wounded him, in an attempt to kill him, as he was trying to save himself from being murdered by them during the fight of Black Jack. I know that for much of the time during the last summer the travel over a portion of the Territory was entirely cut off, and that none but bodies of armed men dared to move at all. I know that for a considerable time the mails on different routes were entirely stopped, and that notwithstanding there were abundant United States troops at hand to escort the mails, such escorts were not furnished as they might or ought to have been. I saw while it was standing, and afterward saw the ruins of, a most valuable house, full of good articles and stores, which had been burned by the ruffians for a highly civilized, intelligent, and most exemplary Christian Indian, for being suspected of favoring Free-State men. He is known as Ottawa Jones, or John T. Jones. In September last I visited a beautiful little Free-State town called Stanton, on the north side of the Osage or Marais des Cygnes River, as it is called, from which every inhabitant had fled (being in fear of their lives), after having built them, at a heavy expense, a strong block-house or wooden fort for their protection. Many of them had left their effects liable to be destroyed or carried off, not being able to remove them. This was a most gloomy scene, and like a visit to a vast sepulchre.

During last summer and fall deserted houses and cornfields were to be met with in almost every direction south of the Kansas River. I saw the burning of Osawatomie by a body of some four hundred ruffians, and of Franklin afterward by some twenty-seven hundred men,— the first-named on August 30, the last-named September 14 or 15. Governor Geary had been for some time in the Territory, and might have saved Franklin with perfect ease. It would not have cost the United States one dollar to have saved Franklin.

I, with five sick and wounded sons and son-in-law, was obliged for some time to lie on the ground, without shelter, our boots and clothes worn out, destitute of money, and at times almost in a state of starvation, and dependent on the charities of the Christian Indian and his wife whom I before named. I saw, in September last, a Mr. Parker, whom I well know, with his head all bruised over and his throat partly cut, having before been dragged, while sick, out of the house of Ottawa Jones, the Indian, when it was burned, and thrown for dead over the bank of the Ottawa Creek.

I saw three mangled bodies of three young men, two of which were dead and had lain on the open ground for about eighteen hours for the flies to work at, the other living with twenty buckshot and bullet-holes in him. One of those two dead was my own son.

6

JOHN BROWN

John Brown's Parallels: Letter to the Editor of the New York Tribune
1859

In October 1858, "Old Osawatomie" John Brown returned to Kansas one last time. The trip was in some ways designed to both confuse his pursuers and remove him from the East, where rumors were circulating that Brown had targeted Appalachia for his next attack. Conditions in the Territory had changed considerably since his last visit: Free staters now controlled the territorial legislature, antislavery settlers were majorities in most counties, and an uneasy peace prevailed. Brown, however, was still determined to strike against slaveholders. On the night of December 20, Brown led a raiding party into Missouri, ransacked two plantations, liberated eleven slaves, and killed a slaveholder. News of the attack spread quickly. President Buchanan offered a $250 reward for Brown's capture (the abolitionist retorted by offering a $2.50 reward for the president's), and the Missouri legislature threatened military action.

Kansas State Historical Society, John Brown Collection, #299, Box 2, Folder 1.

This time, however, Brown's foray alienated free staters. One resident of Trading Post, Kansas, complained that Brown had left bona fide settlers vulnerable to retributive attacks while he himself would be long gone. Brown responded to this line of reasoning and told the story of the raid in an essay entitled "John Brown's Parallels." In the essay, which was published in the New York Tribune, *he justified his attack as retaliation for the Marais des Cygnes massacre of free-state settlers in 1858 and rejoiced that "proslavery, conservative, Free-State, and dough-face men and Administration tools" were filled with "holy horror." Perhaps he believed that if he could ruffle that many feathers with a quick foray into Missouri, his larger plan to attack slavery at its heart—in the mountains of Virginia—would also exceed his expectations.*

On March 12, 1859, after eighty-two days and one thousand miles of hard winter travel, Brown put the liberated slaves (whose number had grown by one due to a baby born en route, not surprisingly christened "John Brown") onto a ferry bound for freedom in Canada. His time in Kansas completed, John Brown returned to the East to plan his final assault on slavery.

TRADING POST, KANSAS, January, 1859.

GENTLEMEN,—YOU will greatly oblige a humble friend by allowing the use of your columns while I briefly state two parallels, in my poor way.

Not one year ago eleven quiet citizens of this neighborhood,— William Robertson, William Colpetzer, Amos Hall, Austin Hall, John Campbell, Asa Snyder, Thomas Stilwell, William Hairgrove, Asa Hairgrove, Patrick Ross, and B. L. Reed,—were gathered up from their work and their homes by an armed force under one Hamilton, and without trial or opportunity to speak in their own defence were formed into line, and all but one shot,—five killed and five wounded. One fell unharmed, pretending to be dead. All were left for dead. The only crime charged against them was that of being Free-State men. Now, I inquire what action has ever, since the occurrence in May last, been taken by either the President of the United States, the Governor of Missouri, the Governor of Kansas, or any of their tools, or by any proslavery or Administration man, to ferret out and punish the perpetrators of this crime?

Now for the other parallel. On Sunday, December 19, a negro man called Jim came over to the Osage settlement, from Missouri, and stated that he, together with his wife, two children, and another negro man, was to be sold within a day or two, and begged for help to get away. On Monday (the following) night, two small companies were made up to go to Missouri and forcibly liberate the five slaves, together with other slaves. One of these companies I assumed to direct. We proceeded to the place, surrounded the buildings, liberated the slaves, and also took certain property supposed to belong to the estate. We however learned before leaving that a portion of the articles we had taken belonged to a man living on the plantation as a tenant, and who was supposed to have no interest in the estate. We promptly returned to him all we had taken. We then went to another plantation, where we found five more slaves, took some property and two white men. We moved all slowly away into the Territory for some distance, and then sent the white men back, telling them to follow us as soon as they chose to do so. The other company freed one female slave, took some property, and, as I am informed, killed one white man (the master), who fought against the liberation.

Now for a comparison. Eleven persons are forcibly restored to their natural and inalienable rights, with but one man killed, and all "hell is stirred from beneath." It is currently reported that the Governor of Missouri has made a requisition upon the Governor of Kansas for the delivery of all such as were concerned in the last-named "dreadful out-rage." The Marshal of Kansas is said to be collecting a *posse* of Missouri (not Kansas) men at West Point, in Missouri, a little town about ten miles distant, to "enforce the laws." All proslavery, conservative, Free-State, and dough-face men and Administration tools are filled with holy horror.

Consider the two cases, and the action of the Administration party.

Respectfully yours,

JOHN BROWN

2

The Raid and Trial

7

JOHN BROWN

Provisional Constitution and Ordinances for the People of the United States

May 8, 1858

In January 1858, Brown visited the Rochester, New York, home of Frederick Douglass. His purpose was to enlist the famous black abolitionist's support for his plan to invade the slave South and wage a guerilla war from a base in the Appalachian Mountains. Douglass's reaction was supportive but cool. During his days at the Douglass home, Brown began composing a "Provisional Constitution" for the new "state" that he hoped to found high in the Appalachian chain. To ratify the new Provisional Constitution, Brown called for a convention to meet in Chatham, Ontario, in May 1858. Chatham was home to a large free black community, many members of which were fugitives from slavery in the United States who had built a new life in Canada. Many of these residents, including the free-born Osborne P. Anderson (see Document 8), were delegates at the convention. Also present were the radical black abolitionist Martin Delany and several Brown allies, including John H. Kagi, Richard Realf, Charles Tidd, Aaron Stevens, J. S. Parsons, and Brown's son Owen. At the convention John Brown, for the first time, laid out his plan to attack slavery by invading the Blue Ridge Mountains in Virginia and waging war on plantations on both sides of the range.

Richard J. Hinton, *John Brown and His Men* (New York: Funk & Wagnalls Co., 1894), 619–33.

After taking an oath of secrecy, the delegates heard each of the forty-eight articles in Brown's Provisional Constitution. Taken as a whole, the document provides a mocking tribute to the U.S. Constitution, which it resembled in most instances. The new constitution, for example, provided for three branches of government, including a commander in chief for the armed forces (Brown). But in the preamble Brown declared slavery, as enshrined in the U.S. Constitution, to be "in utter disregard and violation of those eternal and self-evident truths set forth in our Declaration of Independence." In other articles, the constitution declared that all slaveholders' property would be confiscated, set out punishments for various crimes, and defined plans to hold all property in common. The only item that elicited heated debate was Article XLVI, which stated that the document should not be "construed so as in any way to encourage the overthrow of any State Government of the United States: and look to no dissolution of the Union." The delegates unanimously approved and signed the constitution, agreeing to fill vacancies at a later time. Brown had achieved his goal, and he turned to preparing his invasion.

Preamble

Whereas slavery, throughout its entire existence in the United States, is none other than a most barbarous, unprovoked, and unjustifiable war of one portion of its citizens upon another portion—the only conditions of which are perpetual imprisonment and hopeless servitude or absolute extermination—in utter disregard and violation of those eternal and self-evident truths set forth in our Declaration of Independence:

Therefore we, citizens of the United States, and the oppressed people who, by a recent decision of the Supreme Court, are declared to have no rights which the white man is bound to respect, together with all other people degraded by the laws thereof, do, for the time being, ordain and establish for ourselves the following Provisional Constitution and Ordinances, the better to protect our persons, property, lives, and liberties, and to govern our actions:

Article I: Qualifications for Membership

All persons of mature age, whether proscribed, oppressed, and enslaved citizens, or of the proscribed and oppressed races of the United States, who shall agree to sustain and enforce the Provisional Constitution and Ordinances of this organization, together with all minor children of such persons, shall be held to be fully entitled to protection under the same. . . .

Article XXVIII: Property

All captured or confiscated property, and all property the product of the labor of those belonging to this organization and of their families, shall be held as the property of the whole, equally, without distinction; and may be used for the common benefit, or disposed of for the same object; and any person, officer or otherwise, who shall improperly retain, secret, use or needlessly destroy such property, or property found, captured, or confiscated, belonging to the enemy, or shall willfully neglect to render a full and fair statement of such property by him so taken or held, shall be deemed guilty of a misdemeanor and, on conviction, shall be punished accordingly.

Article XXIX: Safety or Intelligence Fund

All money, plate, watches, or jewelry, captured by honorable warfare, found, taken, or confiscated, belonging to the enemy, shall be held sacred, to constitute a liberal safety or intelligence fund; and any person who shall improperly retain, dispose of, hide, use, or destroy such money or other article above named, contrary to the provisions and spirit of this article, shall be deemed guilty of theft, and, on conviction, thereof, shall be punished accordingly. The Treasurer shall furnish the Commander-in-Chief at all times with a full statement of the condition of such fund and its nature. . . .

Article XXXIII: Voluntaries

All persons who may come forward and shall voluntarily deliver up their slaves, and have their names registered on the Books of the organization, shall, so long as they continue at peace, be entitled to the fullest protection of person and property, though not connected with this organization, and shall be treated as friends, and not merely as persons neutral.

Article XXXIV: Neutrals

The persons and property of all non-slaveholders who shall remain absolute[ly] neutral, shall be respected so far as the circumstances can allow it; but they shall not be entitled to any active protection.

Article XXXV: No Needless Waste

The needless waste or destruction of any useful property or article, by fire, throwing open of fences, fields, buildings, or needless killing of animals, or injury of either, shall not be tolerated at any time or place, but shall be promptly and properly finished.

Article XXXVI: Property Confiscated

The entire and real property of all persons known to be acting either directly or indirectly with or for the enemy, or found in arms with them, or found willfully holding slaves, shall be confiscated and taken, whenever and wherever it may be found, in either free or slave States. . . .

Article XXXIX: All Must Labor

All persons connected in any way with this organization, and who may be entitled to full protection under it: shall be held as under obligation to labor in some way for the general good; and persons refusing, or neglecting so to do, shall on conviction receive a suitable and appropriate punishment.

Article XL: Irregularities

Profane swearing, filthy conversation, indecent behavior, or indecent exposure of the person, or intoxication, or quarrelling, shall not be allowed or tolerated; neither unlawful intercourse of the sexes.

Article XLI: Crimes

Persons convicted of the forcible violation of any female prisoner shall be put to death.

Article XLII: The Marriage Relation — Schools — the Sabbath

The marriage relation shall be at all times respected; and families kept together as far as possible; and broken families encouraged to re-unite, and intelligence offices established for that purpose, schools and churches established, as soon as may be, for the purpose of religious and other instructions and the first day of the week regarded as a day of rest and appropriated to moral and religious instruction and improvement; relief to the suffering, instruction of the young and ignorant, and the encouragement of personal cleanliness nor shall any persons [be] required on that day to perform ordinary manual labor, unless in extremely urgent cases.

Article XLIII: Carry Arms Openly

All persons known to be of good character, and of sound mind and suitable age, who are connected with this organization, whether male or female, shall be encouraged to carry arms openly. . . .

Article XLV: Persons to Be Seized

Persons within the limits of the territory holden by this organization, not connected with this organization, having arms at all, concealed or otherwise, shall be seized at once; or be taken in charge of some vigilant officer; and their case thoroughly investigated: and it shall be the duty of all citizens and soldiers, as well as officers, to arrest such parties as are named in this and the preceding Section or Article, without the formality of complaint or warrant: and they shall be placed in charge of some proper officer for examination, or for safe keeping.

Article XLVI: These Articles Not for the Overthrow of Gov'm't

The foregoing Articles shall not be construed so as in any way to encourage the overthrow of any State Government of the United States: and look to no dissolution of the Union, but simply to Amendment and Repeal. And our flag shall be the same that our Fathers fought under in the Revolution. . . .

Article XLVIII: Oath

Every officer, civil or military, connected with this organization, shall, before entering upon the duties of his office, make solemn oath or affirmation, to abide by and support this Provisional Constitution and these Ordinances. Also, every Citizen and Soldier, before being fully recognized as such, shall do the same.

8

OSBORNE ANDERSON

A Voice from Harpers Ferry

1861

Osborne Perry Anderson, the sole African American survivor of John Brown's raid on Harpers Ferry, provided a unique written account of the planning and execution of the mission. He was born free in Chester County, Pennsylvania, in 1830 and attended Oberlin College in Ohio, a school dedicated to antiracism and coeducation long connected to the abolitionist movement. In 1850, Anderson migrated to Canada, where he became a printer. He met John Brown at the Chatham convention to ratify the Provisional Constitution (see Document 7), where he was named recording secretary for some of the secret proceedings and, later, a member of the provisional congress.

In A Voice from Harpers Ferry, Anderson vividly described the raid from a participant's perspective. On the first night of the raid, Brown ordered Anderson and Albert Hazlett to guard a key position at the arsenal in the town, and when it became clear that the raid was doomed to failure, both men escaped. Hazlett was later captured and executed, but Anderson eluded his pursuers and made his way to Philadelphia, where friends along the Underground Railroad helped him return to Canada.

Because he feared capture as a fugitive from Harpers Ferry, Anderson stayed underground, giving lectures to abolitionist groups and raising money for the publication of his account of the raid, which failed to reach a wide readership.

During the Civil War, Anderson served as a noncommissioned officer in the Union Army, where his very presence (along with 180,000 other black troops) helped make the conflict a war for human freedom. In 1871, he died of tuberculosis at the age of forty-one in Washington, D.C.

Osborne P. Anderson, *A Voice from Harpers Ferry* (Boston: Printed for the Author, 1861), 28–45.

In the evening, before setting out to the Ferry, he [Brown] gave his final charge, in which he said, among other things:—"And now, gentlemen, let me impress this one thing upon your minds. You all know how dear life is to you, and how dear your life is to your friends. And in remembering that, consider that the lives of others are as dear to them as yours are to you. Do not, therefore, take the life of any one, if you can possibly avoid it; but if it is necessary to take life in order to save your own, then make sure work of it."

At eight o'clock on Sunday evening, Captain Brown said: "Men, get on your arms; we will proceed to the Ferry." His horse and wagon were brought out before the door, and some pikes, a sledge-hammer and crowbar were placed in it. The Captain then put on his old Kansas cap, and said: "Come, boys!" when we marched out of the camp behind him, into the lane leading down the hill to the main road. As we formed the procession line, Owen Brown, Barclay Coppic, and Francis J. Merriam, sentinels left behind to protect the place as before stated, came forward and took leave of us; after which, agreeably to previous orders, and as they were better acquainted with the topography of the Ferry, and to effect the tearing down of the telegraph wires, C. P. Tidd and John E. Cook led the procession. While going to the Ferry, the company marched along as solemnly as a funeral procession, till we got to the bridge. When we entered, we halted, and carried out an order to fasten our cartridge boxes outside of our clothes, when every thing was ready for taking the town. . . .

As John H. Kagi and A. D. Stevens entered the bridge, the watchman, being at the other end, came toward them with a lantern in his hand. When up to them, they told him he was their prisoner, and detained him a few minutes, when he asked them to spare his life. They replied, they did not intend to harm him; the object was to free the slaves, and he would have to submit to them for a time, in order that the purpose might be carried out.

Captain Brown now entered the bridge in his wagon, followed by the rest of us, until we reached that part where Kagi and Stevens held their prisoner, when he ordered Watson Brown and Stewart Taylor to take the positions assigned them in order sixth, and the rest of us to proceed to the engine house. We started for the engine house, taking the prisoner along with us. When we neared the gates of the engine-house yard, we found them locked, and the watchman on the inside. He was told to open the gates, but refused, and commenced to cry. The men were then ordered by Captain Brown to open the gates forcibly, which was done, and the watchman taken prisoner. The two prisoners were left in the custody of Jerry Anderson and Adolphus Thompson, and A. D. Stevens arranged the men to take possession of the Armory and rifle factory. About this time, there was apparently much excitement. People were passing back and forth in the town, and before we could do much, we had to take several prisoners. After the prisoners were secured, we passed to the opposite side of the street and took the Armory, and Albert Hazlett and Edwin Coppic were ordered to hold it for the time being.

The capture of the rifle factory was the next work to be done. When we went there, we told the watchman who was outside of the building our business, and asked him to go along with us, as we had come to take possession of the town, and make use of the Armory in carrying out our object. He obeyed the command without hesitation. John H. Kagi and John Copeland were placed in the Armory, and the prisoners taken to the engine house. Following the capture of the Armory, Oliver Brown and William Thompson were ordered to take possession of the bridge leading out of town, across the Shenandoah river, which they immediately did. These places were all taken, and the prisoners secured, without the snap of a gun, or any violence whatever.

The town being taken, Brown, Stevens, and the men who had no post in charge, returned to the engine house, where council was held, after which Captain Stevens, Tidd, Cook, Shields Green, Leary and myself went to the country. On the road, we met some colored men, to whom we made known our purpose, when they immediately agreed to join us. They said they had been long waiting for an opportunity of the kind. Stevens then asked them to go around among the colored people and circulate the news, when each started off in a different direction. . . .

One old colored lady, at whose house we stopped, a little way from the town, had a good time over the message we took her. This liberating the slaves was the very thing she had longed for, prayed for, and dreamed about, time and again; and her heart was full of rejoicing over the fulfilment of a prophecy which had been her faith for long years. While we were absent from the Ferry, the train of cars for Baltimore arrived, and was detained. A colored man named Haywood, employed upon it, went from the Wager House[1] up to the entrance to the bridge, where the train stood, to assist with the baggage. He was ordered to stop by the sentinels stationed at the bridge, which he

---

[1]A hotel near the railroad station.

refused to do, but turned to go in an opposite direction, when he was fired upon, and received a mortal wound. Had he stood when ordered, he would not have been harmed. No one knew at the time whether he was white or colored, but his movements were such as to justify the sentinels in shooting him, as he would not stop when commanded. The first firing happened at that time, and the only firing, until after daylight on Monday morning.

Monday, the 17th of October, was a time of stirring and exciting events. In consequence of the movements of the night before, we were prepared for commotion and tumult, but certainly not for more than we beheld around us. Gray dawn and yet brighter daylight revealed great confusion, and as the sun arose, the panic spread like wild-fire....

Capt. Brown next ordered me to take the pikes out of the wagon in which he rode to the Ferry, and to place them in the hands of the colored men who had come with us from the plantations, and others who had come forward without having had communication with any of our party. It was out of the circumstances connected with the fulfilment of this order, that the false charge against "Anderson" as leader, or "ring-leader," of the negroes, grew.

The spectators, about this time, became apparently wild with fright and excitement. The number of prisoners was magnified to hundreds, and the judgment-day could not have presented more terrors, in its awful and certain prospective punishment to the justly condemned for the wicked deeds of a life-time, the chief of which would no doubt be slaveholding, than did Capt. Brown's operations. why?

The prisoners were also terror-stricken. Some wanted to go home to see their families, as if for the last time. The privilege was granted them, under escort, and they were brought back again. Edwin Coppic, one of the sentinels at the Armory gate, was fired at by one of the citizens, but the ball did not reach him, when one of the insurgents close by put up his rifle, and made the enemy bite the dust....

It was about twelve o'clock in the day when we were first attacked by the troops. Prior to that, Capt. Brown, in anticipation of further trouble, had girded to his side the famous sword taken from Col. Lewis Washington the night before, and with that memorable weapon, he commanded his men against General Washington's own State.

When the Captain received the news that the troops had entered the bridge from the Maryland side, he, with some of his men, went into the street, and sent a message to the Arsenal for us to come forth also. We hastened to the street as ordered, when he said—"The troops are on the bridge, coming into town; we will give them a warm reception." He then walked around amongst us, giving us words of encouragement, in this wise:—"Men! be cool! Don't waste your powder and shot! Take aim, and make every shot count!" "The troops will look for us to retreat on their first appearance; be careful to shoot first." Our men were well supplied with firearms, but Capt. Brown had no rifle at that time; his only weapon was the sword before mentioned.

The troops soon came out of the bridge, and up the street facing us, we occupying an irregular position. When they got within sixty or seventy yards, Capt. Brown said, "Let go upon them!" which we did, when several of them fell. Again and again the dose was repeated.

There was now consternation among the troops. From marching in solid martial columns, they became scattered. Some hastened to seize upon and bear up the wounded and dying,—several lay dead upon the ground. They seemed not to realize, at first, that we would fire upon them, but evidently expected we would be driven out by them without firing. Capt. Brown seemed fully to understand the matter, and hence, very properly and in our defence, undertook to forestall their movements. The consequence of their unexpected reception was, after leaving several of their dead on the field, they beat a confused retreat into the bridge, and there stayed under cover until reinforcements came to the Ferry.

On the retreat of the troops, we were ordered back to our former post. While going, Dangerfield Newby, one of our colored men, was shot through the head by a person who took aim at him from a brick store window, on the opposite side of the street, and who was there for the purpose of firing upon us. Newby was a brave fellow. He was one of my comrades at the Arsenal. He fell at my side, and his death was promptly avenged by Shields Green, the Zouave of the band, who afterwards met his fate calmly on the gallows, with John Copeland. Newby was shot twice; at the first fire, he fell on his side and returned it; as he lay, a second shot was fired, and the ball entered his head. Green raised his rifle in an instant, and brought down the cowardly murderer, before the latter could get his gun back through the sash. . . .

One of the Captain's plans was to keep up communication between his three points. In carrying out this idea, Jerry Anderson went to the rifle factory, to see Kagi and his men. Kagi, fearing that we would be overpowered by numbers if the Captain delayed leaving, sent word by Anderson, to advise him to leave the town at once. This word Anderson communicated to the Captain, and told us also at the Arsenal. The message sent back to Kagi was, to hold out for a few minutes longer, when we would all evacuate the place. Those few minutes proved disastrous, for then it was that the troops before spoken of came pouring in, increased by crowds of men from the surrounding country. After an hour's hard fighting, and when the enemy were blocking up the avenues of escape, Capt. Brown sent out his son Watson with a flag or truce, but no respect was paid to it; he was fired upon, and wounded severely. He returned to the engine house, and fought bravely after that for fully an hour and a half, when he received a mortal wound, which he struggled under until the next day. The contemptible and savage manner in which the flag of truce had been received, induced severe measures in our defence, in the hour and a half before the next one was sent out. The effect of our work was, that the troops ceased to fire at the buildings, as we clearly had the advantage of position.

Capt. A. D. Stevens was next sent out with a flag, with what success I will presently show. Meantime, Jeremiah Anderson, who had brought the message from Kagi previously, was sent by Capt. Brown with another message to John Henrie [sic], but before he got far on the street, he was fired upon and wounded. He returned at once to the engine house, where he survived but a short time. The ball, it was found, had entered the right side in such manner that death necessarily ensued speedily.

Capt. Stevens was fired upon several times while carrying his flag of truce, and received severe wounds, as I was informed that day, not being myself in a position to see him after. He was captured, and taken to the Wager House, where he was kept until the close of the struggle in the evening, when he was placed with the rest of our party who had been captured.

After the capture of Stevens, desperate fighting was done by both sides. . . .

The climax of murderous assaults on that memorable day was the final capture of the engine house, with the old Captain and his handful of associates. This outrageous burlesque upon civilized warfare must have a special chapter to itself, as it concentrates more of Southern littleness and cowardice than is often believed to be true. . . .

Captain Hazlett and myself being in the Arsenal opposite, saw the charge upon the engine house with the ladder, which resulted in opening the doors to the marines, and finally in Brown's capture. The old hero and his men were hacked and wounded with indecent rage, and at last brought out of the house and laid prostrate upon the ground, mangled and bleeding as they were. A formal surrender was required of Captain Brown, which he refused, knowing how little favor he

would receive, if unarmed, at the hands of that infuriated mob. All of
our party who went from the Farm, save the Captain, Shields Green,
Edwin Coppic and Watson Brown, (who had received a mortal wound
some time before,) the men at the Farm, and Hazlett and I, were
either dead or captured before this time; the particulars of whose fate
we learned still later in the day, as I shall presently show. Of the four
prisoners taken at the engine house, Shields Green, the most inex-
orable of all our party, a very Turco in his hatred against the stealers
of men, was under Captain Hazlett, and consequently of our little band
at the Arsenal; but when we were ordered by Captain Brown to return
to our positions, after having driven the troops into the bridge, he mis-
took the order, and went to the engine house instead of with his own
party. Had he remained with us, he might have eluded the vigilant Virginians. As it was, he was doomed, as is well-known, and became a
free-will offering for freedom, with his comrade, John Copeland. Wiser
and better men no doubt there were, but a braver man never lived
than Shields Green.

9

JOHN BROWN

Interview with Senator James Mason, Representative Clement Vallandigham, and Others

October 18, 1859

*After John Brown's surrender in the engine house at Harpers Ferry, the
unconscious, bloody, and wounded raider was moved to the floor of a
paymaster's office in the nearby armory. The next day, Virginia Governor
Henry Wise, U.S. Senator James Mason, Lieutenant J. E. B. Stuart, and
Representatives Clement Vallandigham and Charles Faulkner encircled
Brown's coarse pallet to pummel him with questions. According to Vallandigham, Brown was "anxious to talk and ready to answer anyone
who chose to ask a question."*

New York Herald, October 21, 1859, reprinted with minor variations in Sanborn, *Life and
Letters of John Brown*, 562–69.

Brown was remarkably astute during this three-hour question-and-answer session, but he was not about to answer all of the questions hurled at him. He steadfastly refused to divulge the identities of his collaborators and coconspirators, even though he had left a cache of revealing documents behind at the Kennedy farm. The raid had ended only hours before, but Brown had already moved on to the next—and final— phase of his life: that of an antislavery martyr.

Senator Mason: Can you tell us who furnished money for your expedition?

John Brown: I furnished most of it myself; I cannot implicate others. It is by my own folly that I have been taken. I could easily have saved myself from it, had I exercised my own better judgment rather than yielded to my feelings.

Mason: You mean if you had escaped immediately?

Brown: No. I had the means to make myself Secure without any escape; but I allowed myself to be surrounded by a force by being too tardy. I should have gone away; but I had thirty odd prisoners, whose wives and daughters were in tears for their safety, and I felt for them. Besides, I wanted to allay the fears of those who believed we came here to burn and kill. For this reason I allowed the train to cross the bridge, and gave them full liberty to pass on. I did it only to spare the feelings of those passengers and their families, and to allay the apprehensions that you had got here in your vicinity a band of men who had no regard for life and property, nor any feelings of humanity.

Mason: But you killed some people passing along the streets quietly.

Brown: Well, sir, if there was anything of that kind done, it was without my knowledge. Your own citizens who were my prisoners will tell you that every possible means was taken to prevent it. I did not allow my men to fire when there was danger of killing those we regarded as innocent persons, if I could help it. They will tell you that we allowed ourselves to be fired at repeatedly, and did not return it.

A Bystander: That is not so. You killed an unarmed man at the corner of the house over there at the water-tank, and another besides.

Brown: See here, my friend; it is useless to dispute or contradict the report of your own neighbors who were my prisoners.

Mason: If you would tell us who sent you here,—who provided the means,—that would be information of some value.

Brown: I will answer freely and faithfully about what concerns myself,—I will answer anything I can with honor,—but not about others.

Mr. Vallandigham (who had just entered): Mr. Brown, who sent you here?

Brown: No man sent me here; it was my own prompting and that of my Maker, or that of the Devil,—whichever you please to ascribe it to. I acknowledge no master in human form.

Vallandigham: Did you get up the expedition yourself?

Brown: I did.

Vallandigham: Did you get up this document that is called a Constitution?[1]

Brown: I did. They are a constitution and ordinances of my own contriving and getting up.

Vallandigham: How long have you been engaged in this business?

Brown: From the breaking out of the difficulties in Kansas. Four of my sons had gone there to settle, and they induced me to go. I did not go there to settle, but because of the difficulties.

Mason: How many are there engaged with you in this movement?

Brown: Any questions that I can honorably answer I will,—not otherwise. So far as I am myself concerned, I have told everything truthfully. I value my word, sir.

Mason: What was your object in coming?

Brown: We came to free the slaves, and only that.

A Volunteer: How many men, in all, had you?

Brown: I came to Virginia with eighteen men only, besides myself.

Volunteer: What in the world did you suppose you could do here in Virginia with that amount of men?

Brown: Young man, I do not wish to discuss that question here.

Volunteer: You could not do anything.

Brown: Well, perhaps your ideas and mine on military subjects would differ materially.

Mason: How do you justify your acts?

Brown: I think, my friend, you are guilty of a great wrong against God and humanity,—I say it without wishing to be offensive,—and it would be perfectly right for any one to interfere with you so far as to free those you wilfully and wickedly hold in bondage. I do not say this insultingly.

Mason: I understand that.

[1]See Document 7.

Brown: I think I did right, and that others will do right who interfere with you at any time and at all times. I hold that the Golden Rule, "Do unto others as ye would that others should do unto you," applies to all who would help others to gain their liberty.

Lieutenant Stuart: But don't you believe in the Bible?

Brown: Certainly I do.

. . .

Mason: Did you consider this a military organization in this Constitution? I have not yet read it.

Brown: I did, in some sense. I wish you would give that paper close attention.

Mason: You consider yourself the commander-in-chief of these "provisional" military forces?

Brown: I was chosen, agreeably to the ordinance of a certain document, commander-in-chief of that force.

Mason: What wages did you offer?

Brown: None.

Stuart: "The wages of sin is death."[2]

Brown: I would not have made such a remark to you if you had been a prisoner, and wounded, in my hands.

A Bystander: Did you not promise a negro in Gettysburg twenty dollars a month?

Brown: I did not.

Mason: Does this talking annoy you?

Brown: Not in the least.

Vallandigham: Have you lived long in Ohio?

Brown: I went there in 1805. I lived in Summit County, which was then Portage County. My native place is Connecticut; my father lived there till 1805.

Vallandigham: Have you been in Portage County lately?

Brown: I was there in June last.

Vallandigham: When in Cleveland, did you attend the Fugitive Slave Law Convention there?

Brown: No. I was there about the time of the sitting of the court to try the Oberlin rescuers. I spoke there publicly on that subject; on the Fugitive Slave Law and my own rescue. Of course, so far as I had any influence at all, I was supposed to justify the Oberlin people for

[2] A biblical quotation (Romans 6:23).

rescuing the slave, because I have myself forcibly taken slaves from bondage. I was concerned in taking eleven slaves from Missouri to Canada last winter. I think I spoke in Cleveland before the Convention. I do not know that I had conversation with any of the Oberlin rescuers. I was sick part of the time I was in Ohio with the ague,[3] in Ashtabula County.

Vallandigham: Did you see anything of [antislavery Congressman] Joshua R. Giddings there?

Brown: I did meet him.

Vallandigliam: Did you converse with him?

Brown: I did. I would not tell you, of course, anything that would implicate Mr. Giddings; but I certainly met with him and had conversations with him.

Vallandigliam: About that rescue case?

Brown: Yes; I heard him express his opinions upon it very freely and frankly.

Vallandigham: Justifying it?

Brown: Yes, sir; I do not compromise him, certainly, in saying that.

Vallandigham: Will you answer this: Did you talk with Giddings about your expedition here?

Brown: No, I won't answer that; because a denial of it I would not make, and to make any affirmation of it I should be a great dunce.

Vallandigham: Have you had any correspondence with parties at the North on the subject of this movement?

Brown: I have had correspondence.

A Bystander: Do you consider this a religious movement?

Brown: It is, in my opinion, the greatest service man can render to God.

Bystander: Do you consider yourself an instrument in the hands of Providence?

Brown: I do.

Bystander: Upon what principle do you justify your acts?

Brown: Upon the Golden Rule. I pity the poor in bondage that have none to help them: that is why I am here; not to gratify any personal animosity, revenge, or vindictive spirit. It is my sympathy with the oppressed and the wronged, that are as good as you and as precious in the sight of God.

Bystander: Certainly. But why take the slaves against their will?

Brown: I never did.

Bystander: You did in one instance, at least. [Aaron] Stephens, the other wounded prisoner, here said, "You are right. In one case I know the negro wanted to go back."

[3]Fever.

Bystander. Where did you come from?

Stephens: I lived in Ashtabula County, Ohio.

Vallandigham: How recently did you leave Ashtabula County?

Stephens: Some months ago. I never resided there any length of time; have been through there.

Vallandigham: How far did you live from Jefferson?

Brown: Be cautious, Stephens, about any answers that would commit any friend. I would not answer that.

[Stephens turned partially over with a groan of pain, and was silent.]

Vallandigham: Who are your advisers in this movement?

Brown: I cannot answer that. I have numerous sympathizers throughout the entire North.

Vallandigham: In northern Ohio?

Brown: No more there than anywhere else; in all the free States.

Vallandigham: But you are not personally acquainted in southern Ohio?

Brown: Not very much.

A Bystander. Did you ever live in Washington City?

Brown: I did not. I want you to understand, gentlemen, and [to the reporter of the "Herald"] you may report that,—I want you to understand that I respect the rights of the poorest and weakest of colored people, oppressed by the slave system, just as much as I do those of the most wealthy and powerful. That is the idea that has moved me, and that alone. We expected no reward except the satisfaction of endeavoring to do for those in distress and greatly oppressed as we would be done by. The cry of distress of the oppressed is my reason, and the only thing that prompted me to come here.

Bystander. Why did you do it secretly?

Brown: Because I thought that necessary to success; no other reason.

Bystander. Have you read Gerrit Smith's last letter?

Brown: What letter do you mean?

Bystander. The "New York Herald" of yesterday, in speaking of this affair, mentions a letter in this way:—

> Apropos of this exciting news, we recollect a very significant passage in one of Gerrit Smith's letters, published a month or two ago, in which he speaks of the folly of attempting to strike the shackles off the slaves by the force of moral suasion or legal agitation, and predicts that the next movement made in the direction of negro emancipation would be an insurrection in the South.

Brown: I have not seen the "New York Herald" for some days past; but I presume, from your remark about the gist of the letter, that I should concur with it. I agree with Mr. Smith that moral suasion is hopeless. I don't think the people of the slave States will ever consider the subject of slavery in its true light till some other argument is resorted to than moral suasion.

Vallandigham: Did you expect a general rising of the slaves in case of your success?

Brown: No, sir; nor did I wish it. I expected to gather them up from time to time, and set them free.

Vallandigham: Did you expect to hold possession here till then?

Brown: Well, probably I had quite a different idea. I do not know that I ought to reveal my plans. I am here a prisoner and wounded, because I foolishly allowed myself to be so. You overrate your strength in supposing I could have been taken if I had not allowed it. I was too tardy after commencing the open attack—in delaying my movements through Monday night, and up to the time I was attacked by the Government troops. It was all occasioned by my desire to spare the feelings of my prisoners and their families and the community at large. I had no knowledge of the shooting of the negro Heywood.

Vallandigham: What time did you commence your organization in Canada?

Brown: That occurred about two years ago; in 1858.

Vallandigham: Who was the secretary?

Brown: That I would not tell if I recollected; but I do not recollect. I think the officers were elected in May, 1858. I may answer incorrectly, but not intentionally. My head is a little confused by wounds, and my memory obscure on dates, etc.

Dr. Biggs: Were you in the party at Dr. Kennedy's house?

Brown: I was the head of that party. I occupied the house to mature my plans. I have not been in Baltimore to purchase caps.

Dr. Biggs: What was the number of men at Kennedy's?

Brown: I decline to answer that.

Dr. Biggs: Who lanced that woman's neck on the hill?

Brown: I did. I have sometimes practised in surgery when I thought it a matter of humanity and necessity, and there was no one else to do it; but I have not studied surgery.

Dr. Biggs: It was done very well and scientifically. They have been very clever to the neighbors, I have been told, and we had no reason to suspect them, except that we could not understand their movements. They were represented as eight or nine persons; on Friday there were thirteen.

Brown: There were more than that.

Q: Where did you get arms? *A*. I bought them.

Q: In what State? *A*. That I will not state.

Q: How many guns? *A*. Two hundred Sharpe's rifles and two hundred revolvers,—what is called the Massachusetts Arms Company's revolvers, a little under navy size.

Q: Why did you not take that swivel[4] you left in the house? *A*. I had no occasion for it. It was given to me a year or two ago.

Q: In Kansas? *A*. No. I had nothing given to me in Kansas.

Q: By whom, and in what State? *A*. I decline to answer. It is not properly a swivel; it is a very large rifle with a pivot. The ball is larger than a musket ball; it is intended for a slug.

Reporter: I do not wish to annoy you; but if you have anything further you would like to say, I will report it.

Brown: I have nothing to say, only that I claim to be here in carrying out a measure I believe perfectly justifiable, and not to act the part of an incendiary or ruffian, but to aid those suffering great wrong. I wish to say, furthermore, that you had better—all you people at the South—prepare yourselves for a settlement of this question, that must come up for settlement sooner than you are prepared for it. The sooner you are prepared the better. You may dispose of me very easily,—I am nearly disposed of now; but this question is still to be settled,—this negro question I mean; the end of that is not yet. These wounds were inflicted upon me—both sabre cuts on my head and bayonet stabs in different parts of my body—some minutes after I had ceased fighting and had consented to surrender, for the benefit of others, not for my own. I believe the Major would not have been alive; I could have killed him just as easy as a mosquito when he came in, but I supposed he only came in to receive our surrender. There had been loud and long calls of "surrender" from us,—as loud as men could yell; but in the confusion and excitement I suppose we were not heard. I do not think the Major, or any one, meant to butcher us after we had surrendered.

An Officer: Why did you not surrender before the attack?

Brown: I did not think it was my duty or interest to do so. We assured the prisoners that we did not wish to harm them, and they should be set at liberty. I exercised my best judgment, not believing the people would wantonly sacrifice their own fellow-citizens, when we offered to let them go on condition of being allowed to change our position about a quarter of a mile. The prisoners agreed by a vote among themselves to pass across the bridge with us. We wanted

[4]A type of small cannon.

them only as a sort of guarantee of our own safety,—that we should not be fired into. We took them, in the first place, as hostages and to keep them from doing any harm. We did kill some men in defending ourselves, but I saw no one fire except directly in self-defence. Our orders were strict not to harm any one not in arms against us.

Q: Brown, suppose you had every nigger in the United States, what would you do with them? *A*. Set them free.

Q: Your intention was to carry them off and free them? *A*. Not at all.

A Bystander: To set them free would sacrifice the life of every man in this community.

Brown: I do not think so.

Bystander: I know it. I think you are fanatical.

Brown: And I think you are fanatical. "Whom the gods would destroy they first make mad," and you are mad.

Q: Was it your only object to free the negroes? *A*. Absolutely our only object.

Q: But you demanded and took Colonel Washington's silver and watch? *A*. Yes; we intended freely to appropriate the property of slaveholders to carry out our object. It was for that, and only that, and with no design to enrich ourselves with any plunder whatever.

Bystander: Did you know Sherrod in Kansas? I understand you killed him.

Brown: I killed no man except in fair fight. I fought at Black Jack Point and at Osawatomie; and if I killed anybody, it was at one of these places.

10

Excerpts from the Trial of John Brown
1859

Barely a week after his capture, John Brown went on trial before circuit court Judge Richard Parker in Charles Town, Virginia. The authorities were terrified that Brown would be either lynched by angry Southerners or broken out of jail by wily abolitionists, so the trial (and, according to many Northerners, the justice) was rushed. All requests for delays were denied, and Brown settled in for what was to be—considering his business failures and blunders as a military tactician, a leader, and a father—his greatest moment. Reporters from all parts of the Union gathered in the Jefferson County courthouse to witness the trial, and Brown, ever mindful of his audience, flawlessly played the part of eloquent martyr. His opening remarks assail the mockery of justice that Brown considered his trial to be and angrily challenge the claims of his insanity offered by his own lawyer. Most significantly, Brown's final address to the court—at a mere five minutes—stands as one of the greatest examples of American oratory. He forcefully restated his intentions, mocked the charges brought against him, and declared that the Bible's Golden Rule forced him to do what he did: "I believe that to have interfered as I have done—in behalf of His despised poor, was not wrong, but right." Then he stood calmly as Judge Parker sentenced him to hang from the neck on December 2, 1859.

Opening Remarks of John Brown to the Virginia Court, October 27, 1859

Virginians, I did not ask for any quarter at the time I was taken. I did not ask to have my life spared. The Governor of the State of Virginia tendered me his assurance that I should have a fair trial; but, under no circumstances whatever, will I be able to have a fair trial. If you seek my blood, you can have it at any moment, without this mockery of a trial. I have had no counsel. I have not been able to advise with any one. I know nothing about the feelings of my fellow-prisoners, and am utterly unable to attend in any way to my own defense. My memory

---

Franklin Sanborn, *Life and Letters of John Brown* (London: Sampson Low, Marson, Searle, & Irvington, 1885), 572–85.

don't serve me. My health is insufficient, though improving. There are mitigating circumstances that I would urge in our favor, if a fair trial is to be allowed us. But if we are to be forced with a mere form—a trial for execution—you might spare yourselves that trouble. I am ready for my fate. I do not ask for a trial. I beg for no mockery of a trial—no insults—nothing but that which conscience gives, or cowardice would drive to practise. I ask again to be excused from the mockery of a trial. . . . I have now little further to ask, other than that I may not be foolishly insulted, only as cowardly barbarians insult those who fall into their power.

John Brown's Response to Claims of His Insanity, October 28, 1859

I look upon it as a miserable artifice and pretext of those who ought to take a different course in regard to me. . . . Insane persons, so as my experience goes, have but little ability to judge of their own sanity; and if I am insane of course I should think I know more than all the rest of the world. But I do not think so. I am perfectly unconscious of insanity, and I reject, so far as I am capable, any attempt to interfere in my behalf on that score.

Last Address of John Brown to the Virginia Court, November 2, 1859

I have, may it please the Court, a few words to say.

In the first place, I deny everything but what I have all along admitted, of a design on my part to free the slaves. I intended certainly to have made a clean thing of that matter, as I did last winter, when I went into Missouri and there took slaves without the snapping of a gun on either side, moved them through the country, and finally left them in Canada. I designed to have done the same thing again, on a larger scale. That was all I intended. I never did intend murder, or treason, or the destruction of property, or to excite or incite slaves to rebellion, or to make insurrection.

I have another objection; and that is, it is unjust that I should suffer such a penalty. Had I interfered in the manner which I admit, and which I admit has been fairly proved (for I admire the truthfulness and candor of the greater portion of the witnesses who have testified in this case),—had I so interfered in behalf of the rich, the powerful, the intelligent, the so-called great, or in behalf of any of their friends,—either father, mother, brother, sister, wife, or children, or any of that class,—and suffered and sacrificed what I have in this interference, it would have been all right; and every man in this court would have deemed it an act worthy of reward rather than punishment.

This court acknowledges, as I suppose, the validity of the law of God. I see a book kissed here which I suppose to be the Bible, or at least the New Testament. That teaches me that all things whatsoever I would that men should do to me, I should do even so to them. It teaches me, further to "remember them that are in bonds, as bound with them." I endeavored to act up to that instruction. I say, I am yet too young to understand that God is any respecter of persons. I believe that to have interfered as I have done—in behalf of His despised poor, was not wrong, but right. Now, if it is deemed necessary that I should forfeit my life for the furtherance of the ends of justice, and mingle my blood further with the blood of my children and with the blood of millions in this slave country whose rights are disregarded by wicked, cruel, and unjust enactments,—I submit; so let it be done!

Let me say one word further.

I feel entirely satisfied with the treatment I have received on my trial. Considering all the circumstances, it has been more generous than I expected. But I feel no consciousness of guilt. I have stated from the first what was my intention, and what was not. I never have had any design against the life of any person, nor any disposition to commit treason, or excite slaves to rebel, or make any general insurrection. I never encouraged any man to do so, but always discouraged any idea of that kind.

Let me say, also, a word in regard to the statements made by some of those connected with me. I hear it has been stated by some of them that I have induced them to join me. But the contrary is true. I do not say this to injure them, but as regretting their weakness. There is not one of them but joined me of his own accord, and the greater part of them at their own expense. A number of them I never saw, and never had a word of conversation with, till the day they came to me; and that was for the purpose I have stated.

Now I have done.

3

The Making of a Martyr

11

JOHN BROWN

Selected Prison Letters
October 21–December 2, 1859

Within moments of hearing his death sentence Brown returned to his cell and began writing letters to family members, supporters, strangers, and newspaper editors. Many of these letters quickly found their way into print and cemented once and for all Brown's status as an abolitionist martyr. In the scores of letters written over the last month of his life, Brown explained and justified his actions at Harpers Ferry, converting many critics into sympathizers. In fact, he did far better in the court of Northern public opinion than he had in Judge Parker's courtroom.

The most striking thing about the collected correspondence is how obviously each letter was intended for a broad (and public) audience. Even his letters to Mary and his children sound as if they had been written for posterity, as well as to comfort loved ones in the loss of their husband and father. Brown saw his opportunity and seized it: "I feel quite determined to make the utmost possible out of a defeat," he told his wife. Mixing his own actions and thoughts with those of Old and New Testament prophets, Brown compared himself variously to the imprisoned Paul, the errant Moses, the tragic Samson, and even the condemned Jesus Christ. In his final letter, written the morning of his execution, he literally became a prophet. A note slipped to one of his guards predicted that "the crimes of this guilty land: will never be purged away; but with

Franklin Sanborn, *Life and Letters of John Brown* (London: Sampson Low, Marson, Searle, & Irvington, 1885), 579–620.

Blood. I had as I now think; vainly *flattered myself that without* very much *bloodshed; it might be done." The strange syntax is no longer that of a failed tanner, a vigilante, or even a grandiose military schemer. John Brown had become a bona fide martyr to the cause of freedom.*

Charlestown, Jefferson Co., Va., 31st Oct. 1859

My dear Wife, and Children every one

I suppose you have learned before this by the newspapers that two weeks ago today we were fighting for our lives at Harpers ferry: that during the fight Watson was mortally wounded; Oliver killed, Wm Thompson killed, & Dauphin slightly wounded. That on the following day I was taken prisoner immediately after which I received several Sabre cuts in my head; & Bayonet stabs in my body. As nearly as I can learn Watson died of his wound on Wednesday the 2d or on Thursday the 3d day after I was taken. Dauphin was killed when I was taken; & Anderson I suppose also. I have since been tried, & found guilty of treason, &c; and of murder in the first degree. I have not yet received my sentence. No others of the company with who you were acquainted were so far as *I can learn* either killed or taken. Under all these terrible calamities; I feel quite cheerful in the assurance that God reigns; & will overrule all for his glory; & the best possible good. I feel *no* con[s]ciou[s]ness of *guilt* in the matter: nor even mortification on account of my imprisonment; & irons; & I feel perfectly assured that very soon no member of my family will feel any possible disposition to "blush on my account." Already dear friends at a distance with kindest sympathy are cheering me with the assurance that *posterity* at least: will do me justice. I shall commend you all together with my beloved; but bereaved daughters in law to their sympathies which I have no doubt will soon reach you. I also commend you all to him "whose mercy endureth forever": to the God of my *fathers* "whose I am; & whom I serve." "He will never leave you or forsake you" unless you forsake him. Finally my dearly beloved be of good comfort. Be as it has been consistent with the holy religion of Jesus Christ in which I remain a most firm, & humble believer. Never forget the poor nor think any thing you bestow on them to be lost to you even though they may be as *black* as Ebedmelch, the Ethiopian eunuch one to whom Phillip preached Christ. Be sure to entertain strangers . . . "Remember them that are in bonds as bound with them." I am in charge of a jailor *like* the one who took charge of "Paul & Silas"; & you may rest assured that both *kind hearts* and *kind faces* are more or less about me: whilst thousands are thirsting for my blood. "These *light* afflictions which are but *for a moment* shall work out for us a far *more exceeding & eternal* weight of glory." I hope to be able to write you again. My wounds are doing well. Copy this & send it to your sorrow stricken brothers, *Ruth*; to comfort them. Write me a few words in regard to the welfare of all. God Almighty bless you all: & make you "joyful in the midst of all your tribulations." Write to John Brown, Charlestown, Jefferson Co, Va, care of Capt John Avis

Your Affectionate Husband, & Father. John Brown

Nov. 3d 1859

P.S. Yesterday Nov 2d I was sentenced to be hanged on 2 Decem next. Do not grieve on my account. I am still quite cheerful.

Go[d] bless you all Your Ever J Brown

———

Charlestown, Jefferson County, Va., Nov. 1, 1859

My Dear Friend E.B. of R.I.,

Your most cheering letter of the 27th of October is received; and may the Lord reward you a thousandfold for the kind feeling you express toward me; but more especially for your fidelity to the "poor that cry, and those that have no help." For this I am a prisoner in bonds. It is solely my own fault, in a military point of view, that we met with our disaster. I mean that I mingled with our prisoners and so far sympathized with them and their families that I neglected my duty in other respects. But God's will, not mine, be done.

You know that Christ once armed Peter. So also in my case I think he put a sword into my hand, and there continued it so long as he saw best, and then kindly took it from me. I mean when I first went to Kansas. I wish you could know with what cheerfulness I am now wielding the "sword of the Spirit" on the right hand and on the left. I bless God that it proves "mighty to the pulling down of strongholds." I always loved my Quaker friends, and I commend to their kind regard my poor bereaved widowed wife and my daughters and daughters-in-law, whose husbands fell at my side. One is a mother and the other likely to become so soon. They, as well as my own sorrow-stricken daughters, are left very poor, and have much greater need of sympathy than I, who, through Infinite Grace and the kindness of strangers, am "joyful in all my tribulations."

Dear sister, write them at North Elba, Essex County, N.Y., to comfort their sad hearts. Direct to Mary A. Brown, wife of John Brown. There is also another—a widow, wife of Thompson, who fell with my poor boys in the affair at Harper's Ferry—at the same place.

I do not feel conscious of guilt in taking up arms; and had it been in behalf of the rich and powerful, the intelligent, the great (as men count greatness), or those who form enactments to suit themselves and corrupt others, or some of their friends, that I interfered, suffered, sacrificed, and fell, it would have been doing very well. But enough of this. These light afflictions, which endure for a moment, shall but work for me "a far more exceeding and eternal weight of glory." I would be very grateful for another letter from you. My wounds are healing. Farewell. God will surely attend to his own cause in the best possible way and time, and he will not forget the work of his own hands.

Your friend, John Brown.

———

Charlestown, Jefferson Co. Va. 4th Nov. 1859

Rev. T. W. Higginson
Dear Friend

If my Wife were to come here just now it would *only tend* to distract *her mind, ten fold*; & would *only add* to my affliction; & cannot *possibly* do me *any good*. It will also use up the scanty means she has to supply Bread & cheap but comfortable clothing, fuel & C) for herself, and Children *through the Winter.* DO PERSUADE her to remain *at home for a time (at least)* till she can learn further from me. She will secure a Thousand times the consolation AT HOME that she can possibly find elsewhere. I have just *written her there & will* write her CONSTANTLY. Her presence *here* will deepen my affliction a thousand fold. I beg of her to be *calm, & submissive*; & not to go *wild* on my account. I lack *for nothing* & was feeling quite cheerful before I learned she talked of *coming on. I ask her to compose her mind* & to remain *quiet* till the last of this *month*; out of pity to me. I can certainly judge better in this matter than *any one else.* My warmest thanks to yourself; & *all other* kind friends. *God bless you all. Please send this line to my afflicted Wife*, by first possible conveyance.

Your friend in truth, John Brown

———

                                    Charlestown, Jefferson Co. Va. 4th Nov. 1859
Mrs L Maria Child, Wayland, Mass
My Dear friend

(Such you prove to be though an entire stranger) Your most kind
letter has reached me; with your kind offer to come here & take care
of me. Allow me to express my gratitude for your great sympathy: &
at the same time to propose to you a different course; together with
my reasons for wishing it. I should certainly be greatly pleased to
become personally acquainted with one so gifted; & so kind; but I cannot avoid seeing some objections to it under present circumstances.
First I am in charge of a most humane gentleman who with his family
have rendered me every possible attention I have desired or that
could be of the least advantage: and I am so far recovered from my
wounds as no longer to require nursing. Then again it would subject
you to great personal inconvenience, & quite a heavy expence; without
doing me any good. Now allow me to name to you another channel
through which you may reach me with your sympathies much more
effectually. I have at home a Wife & three young daughters. The
youngest of whom is but a little over Five years old; the oldest is
nearly Sixteen. I have also two daughters in law whose Husbands have
both fallen near me here. One of these is a Mother & the other like to
become so. There is also another Widow a Mrs. Thompson whose
Husband also fell here. Whether she is a Mother or not I cannot say.
They all (my Wife included) live at North Elba, Essex Co. New York. I
have or suppose I have a middle aged Son who has been in some
degree a cripple from childhood who would have as much as he could
well do to earn a living. He was a most dreadful sufferer in Kansas;
& lost all he had laid up: & has not enough to clothe himself for the
Winter comfortably. I have *no son or son in law living*; who did not suffer terribly in Kansas. Now dear friend would you not as soon con-
tribute Fifty Cents now: & a like sum *yearly* for the relief of those very
poor; & deeply afflicted persons to enable to supply themselves, &
Children with Bread: & very plain clothing; & to enable the children
to receive a common English education: & also to devote your own
energies to induce others to join you in giving a like or other amount
to constitute a little fund for the purpose named? I cannot see how
your coming here can possibly do me the least good: & I feel quite
certain you can do me *immence good* where you are. I am quite cheerful under all my afflicting circumstances; & prospects, having as I
humbly trust "the peace of God which passeth all understanding, to

rule in my heart." You may make just such use of this as you see fit. Yours *in sincerity; & truth*, (God Allmighty bless; and reward you a thousand time fold.)

John Brown

Charlestown, Jefferson Co. Va, 15th Nov. 1859

Rev. H L Vaill
My Dear Stedfast Friend

Your most *kind & most welcome* letter of the 8th inst reached me in due time. *I am very grateful* for all the good feeling you express & also for the kind counsels you give together—with your prayers in my behalf. Allow me here to say notwithstanding "my soul is amongst lions," still I believe that "God in very deed is with me." You will not therefore feel surprised when I tell you that I am "joyful in all my tribulations": that I do not feel condemned of Him whose judgment is just; nor of my own conscience. Nor do I feel degraded by my imprisonment, my chains or prospect of the Gallows. I have not only been (*though utterly unworthy*) permitted to "suffer affliction with God's people," but have also had *a great many rare* opportunities for "preaching *righteousness* in the great congregation." I trust it will not all be lost. *The jailor* (in whose charge I am) *& his family; & assistants* have all been most kind: & notwithstanding he was one of the bravest of all who *fought me*: he is *now* being abused for humanity. So far as my observation goes; *none but brave* men: are likely to be *humane*; to a fallen foe. "Cowards *prove* their *courage* by their *ferocity.*" It may be done in that way with but little risk. I wish I could write you about a few only of the interesting times, I here experience with different classes of men; *clergymen* among others. Christ the great Captain of *liberty*; as well as of salvation; & who began his mission, as foretold of him; by proclaiming it, *saw fit* to take from me a sword of steel after I had carried it for a time but he has put another in my hand ("The sword of the Spirit;") & I pray God to make me a faithful soldier wherever he may send me, not less on the scaffold, then when surrounded by the warmest sympathizers. My dear old friend I do assure you I have not forgotten our last meeting nor our retrospective look over the route by which God had then led us; & I bless his name that he has again enabled me to hear your words of cheering; & comfort, at a time when I at least am on the "brink of Jordan." See Bunyan's

Pilgrim. God in Infinite mercy grant us *soon* another meeting on the opposite shore. I have often passed under the rod of him whom I *call my* Father; & certainly no son ever needed it oftener; & yet I have enjoyed much of life, as I was enabled to discover the secret of this; somewhat early. It has been in making the prosperity, & the happiness of others *my own*: so that really I have had a great deal of prosperity. I am very prosperous still; & looking forward to a time when "peace on Earth & good will to *men* shall every where prevail." I have no murmuring thoughts of *envyous* feelings to fret my mind. "I'll praise my *maker* with my *breath*." I am *an unworthy* nephew of Deacon John; & I loved him much; & in view of the many choice friends *I have had* here I am led the more earnestly to pray; "gather *not* my soul with the *unrighteous*." Your assurance of the earnest sympathy of the friends in my native land is very greatful to my feelings; & allow me to say a word of comfort to them. As I believe most firmly that God reigns; I cannot believe that any thing I have *done suffered or may yet suffer will be lost*; to the *cause of God or of humanity*: & before I began my work at Harpers Ferry; I felt assured that in the *worst event*; it would certainly PAY. I often expressed that belief; & I can now see no possible cause to alter my mind. I am not as yet in the *main* at all disappointed. I have been *a good deal* disappointed as it regards *myself* in not keeping up to *my own plans*; but I now feel entirely reconciled to that even: for Gods plan, was Infinitely better; *no doubt*: or I should have kept to my own. Had Samson kept to his *determination* of not telling Delilah wherein his great strength lay; he would probably have never overturned the house. I did not tell Delilah; but I was induced to act very *contrary* to my *better judgment*: & I have lost my two noble boys; & *other friends, if not my two eyes*.

But "Gods will not *mine* be done." I feel a comfortable hope that like the *erring servant* of whom I have just been writing *even I* may (through Infinite mercy in Christ Jesus) yet "die in faith." As to both the time, & manner of my death: I have but very little trouble on that score; & *am able* to be (as you exhort) "of good cheer." I send through you my best wishes to Mrs. Woodruff & her son George; & to all dear friends. May the God of the *poor* and *oppressed*; be the God & Saveior of you all. Farewell till we "*meet again*."

Your friend in truth, John Brown

Charlestown, Jefferson Co. Va. 19th Nov. 1859

Rev. Luther Humphrey.

My dear friend,

Your kind letter of 12th inst. is now before me. So far as my knowledge goes as to our mutual kindred, I suppose *I am the first* since the landing of Peter Brown from the Mayflower that *has either been sentenced to imprisonment*; or to the Gallows. But my dear old friend, let not that fact *alone* grieve you. You cannot have forgotten *how; & where our Grandfather* (Capt. John Brown) fell in 1776; *& that he too* might have perished on the scaffold had circumstances been but *very little* different. *The fact* that a man dies under the hand of an executioner (or other wise) has but little to do with his true character, as I suppose. John Rogers perished at the stake *a great & good* man as I suppose: but *his being* so does *not prove* that any other man who has died in the same way was *good or otherwise.* Whether I have any reason to "be of good cheer" (or not) in view of my end; I can assure you that *I feel so*; & that I am totally *blinded* if I do not really *experience* that *strengthening*; *& consolation* you so faithfully implore on my behalf. God of *our Fathers*; reward your fidelity. I neither feel *mortified, degraded, nor in the least ashamed* of my imprisonment, my chain, or my prospect of *death by hanging.* I feel assured "that not one hair shall fall from my head without my heavenly Father." I also feel that I have *long been endeavoring* to hold exactly "such a *fast* as God has chosen." See the passage in Isaiah which you have quoted. No part of my life has been more hapily spent; than that I have spent here; & I humbly *trust* that no past has been spent to better purpose. *I would not say boastingly*: but "thanks be unto God who giveth us the victory: *through infinite grace.*" I should be sixty years old were I to live till May 9th 1860. I have enjoyed much of life as it is: & have been remarkably prosperous; having *early learned* to regard the welfare & property of others as *my own.* I have never since I can remember required a great amount of sleep: so that I conclude that I have already enjoyed *full an average* number of waking hours with those who reach their "Three Score years, & ten." I have not as yet been driven to the use of glasses; but can still see to read, & write quite comfortably. But more than that I have *generally* enjoyed remarkably good health. I might go on to recount unnumbered *& unmerited* blessings among which would be some very severe afflictions: & those the most needed blessings of all. And now when I think how easily I might *be left to spoil* all I have done, or suffered in the cause of freedom; I hardly dare risk another voyage; if I even had the opportunity. It is a long time since we met; but we shall now soon come together in our "Father's House," *I trust.* "Let us hold fast that we already have," "remembering that we shall reap in due time if we faint not." Thanks be *ever* unto God; who giveth us the victory through Jesus Christ our Lord." And now my old warm-hearted friend, "Good bye." Your Affectionate Cousin, John Brown

————

Charlestown, Jefferson Co. Va. 22d, Nov. 1859

Rev TW Higginson
Dear Sir

I write you a few lines to express to you my deep feeling of gratitude for your journey to visit & comfort my family as well as myself in different ways & at different times; since *my* imprisonment here. Truly you have proved yourself to be "a friend in need"; & *I feel* my many obligations for all your kind *attentions, none the less*: for my wishing my Wife *not* to come on when she first set out. I would it were in my power to make to *all* my kind friends: some *other acknowledgements* than a mere tender of *our* & *my* thanks. I can assure *all*: Mrs. Stearns, my young friend Hoyt; & many others I have been unable to write as of yet: that I *certainly do not forget*; their love, & kindness. God *Allmighty* bless; & save them *all*; & grant *them to see*; a fulfilment of all their reasonable desires. My daughter writes me that you have sent $25. Twenty Five Dollars in a letter with a bundle of papers. I wish to thank you in particular for sending *them papers*, & hope you will continue this kindness. Friends in the cities who get more papers than they can read; cannot think how much it may add to the comfort of a bereaved family to receive a good paper from time to time from distant friends *even though* those friends may be entire strangers. I am getting much better at my wounds; but am *yet rather lame*. Am very cheerful & *trust* I may continue so "to the end." My Love to all dear friends. Yours for *God & the right*. John Brown

————

Jail, Charlestown, Wednesday, Nov. 23, 1859

Rev. McFarland,
Dear Friend:

Although you write to me as a stranger, the spirit you show towards me and the cause for which I am in bonds, makes me feel towards you as a dear friend. I would be glad to have you, or any of my liberty-loving ministerial friends here, to talk and pray with me. I am not a stranger to the way of salvation by Christ. From my youth I have studied much on that subject, and at one time hoped to be a minister myself; but God had another work for me to do. To me it is given in behalf of Christ, not only to believe in him, but also to *suffer* for his sake. But while I trust that I have some experimental and saving knowledge of religion, it would be a great pleasure to me to have some one better qualified than myself to lead my mind in prayer and meditation, now that my time is so near a close. You may wonder, are there no ministers of the gospel here? I answer, No. There are no ministers of *Christ* here. These ministers who profess to be Christian, and hold slaves or advocate slavery, I cannot abide them. My knees will not bend in prayer with them while their hands are stained with the blood of souls. The subject you mention as having been preaching on, the day before you wrote to me, is one which I have often thought of since my imprisonment. I think I feel as happy as Paul did when he lay in prison. He knew if they killed him it would greatly advance the cause of Christ; that was the reason he rejoiced so. On that same ground "I do rejoice, yea, and will rejoice." Let them hang me; I forgive them, and may God forgive them, for they know not what they do. I have no regret for the transaction for which I am condemned. I went against the laws of men, it is true; but "whether it be right to obey *God* or *men*, judge ye." Christ told me to remember them that are in bonds, as *bound with them*, to do towards them as I would wish them to do towards me in similar circumstances. My conscience bade me do that. I tried to do it, but failed. Therefore I have no regret on that score. I have no sorrow either as to the result, only for my poor wife and children. They have suffered much, and it is hard to leave them uncared for. But God will be a husband to the widow, and a father to the fatherless.

I have frequently been in Wooster; and if any of my old friends from Akron are there, you can show them this letter. I have but a few more days, and I feel anxious to be away, "where the wicked cease from troubling, and the weary are at rest." Farewell.

Your friend, and the friend of all friends of liberty, John Brown.

Charlestown, Jefferson Co. Va. 26th Nov. 1859
(Nov. 27th I mean to write again with some care)

My dear Wife

I wrote our dear friend McKim a few lines yesterday saying I had got his kind letter informing me of where you then were; & how to direct to you while in his neighborhood. I also said to him that I would be glad to have you remain about there; until I was disposed of: *or untill*; I could send you a few little articles by Express: & also write you further; if that (could be) without your becoming burdensome to friends. Our friend McKim wrote me you had gone; *or was going* to stay a while with *Lucretia Mott*. I remember the faithful old Lady well; but presume she has no recollection of me. I once set myself to oppose a *mob* at Boston; where she was. After I interfered the police immediately took up the matter; & soon put a stop to mob proceedings. The meeting was I think in *Marlboro Street* Church, or *Hotel perhaps*. I am glad to have you make the acquaintance of such old "Pioneers" in the cause. I have just received from Mr. John Jay of New York a draft for $50, Fifty Dollars for the benefit of my family; & will enclose *it*; made payable to your order. I have also $15, Fifteen Dollars to send our cripled, & *destitute* unmarried son; when I can I intend to send you by Express Care of Mr. McKim Two or Three little articles to carry home. Should you happen to meet with Mr. Jay say to him that I fully appreciate his great kindness both to *me; & my family*. God bless *all* such friends. It is out of my power to reply to *all* the kind, & encouraging letters *I get*; *Wish* I could do so. I have been so much relieved from my lameness for the last Three or Four days as to be able to sit up to read; & write pretty much all day: as well as part of the Night; & I do assure you & *all other* friends that I am quite busy; & *none the less happy* on that account. The time passes *quite pleasantly*; & the near aproach of my great change is not the occasion of any particular dread. I trust that *God* who has sustained me *so long*; will not *forsake* me when I most feel my need of *Fatherly aid; & support*. Should he hide his face; my spirit will droop, & die: *but not otherwise: be assured*. My only anxiety is to be properly assured of my *fitness* for the company of those who are "washed from *all filthiness*": & *for the presence of Him who is Infinitely pure*. I certainly *think* I do have *some* "hunger, & *thirst* after righteousness." If it be only *genuine* I make *no doubt I "shall be filled."* Please let all our friends read my letters when you can; & ask them to accept of it *as in part for them*. I am inclined to think you will not be likely to succeed well about getting away the bodies of your family; but should that *be so: do not let that grieve you.* It can make but little difference *what is done with them.* I would advise that you take any little funds you may have to carry home in Gold (smallish sized) *in good part;* which some kind friend will obtain at a Bank for you. You can continue to carry (*the most of it*) about your person in some *safe way:* & it will not be best for me to advise you about making the little you now get; reach as far as you consistently can. You can well remember the changes you have passed through. Life is made up of a series of changes: & let us try to meet them in the best maner possible. You will not wish to make yourself & children any more burdensome to friends than you are really compelled to do. *I would not.*

I will close this by saying that if you *now feel* that you are *equal* to the undertaking do *exactly as you FEEL disposed to do* about coming to see me before I suffer. *I am entirely willing.*

Your Affectionate Husband, John Brown

Charlestown, Jefferson Co., Va., Monday, Nov. 28, 1859

Hon. D. R. Tilden.

My Dear Sir,

Your *most kind and comforting* letter of the 23d inst. is received.

I have no language to express the feelings of gratitude and obligation I am under for your kind interest in my behalf ever since my disaster.

The great bulk of mankind estimate each other's actions *and motives* by the measure of success or *otherwise* that attends them through life. By that rule I have been one of the *worst* and one of the *best* of men. I *do* not claim to have been one of the latter; and I leave it to an impartial tribunal to decide whether the world has been the *worse* or the better of my *living* and *dying* in it. My present great anxiety is to get as near in readiness for a different field of action as I well *can* since being in a good measure *relieved from the fear* that my poor, *broken-hearted wife and children* would come to immediate want. May God reward, *a thousand fold,* all the kind efforts made in their behalf. I have enjoyed *remarkable cheerfulness and composure of mind* ever since my confinement; and it is a great comfort to *feel assured* that *I am permitted* to die (for a *cause*) not *merely* to pay the debt of nature, (as all must). I feel myself to be *most* unworthy of so *great* distinction. The particular manner of dying *assigned* to me, gives me but very little *uneasiness.* I wish I had the time and the ability to give you (my dear friend) some little idea of what is *daily, and, I might also say, hourly*, passing within my *prison walls*; and could my friends but witness only a few of those scenes just as they occur, I think they would feel very reconciled to my being here *just what I am, and just as I am.* My *whole* life *before* had not afforded me one half the opportunity to plead *for the right. In this*, also, *I find* much to reconcile me to both my present condition and my immediate prospect. I may be *very insane*, (and I *am so*, if insane at all.) But if that be so, *insanity* is like a very pleasant dream to me. I am not in the least degree conscious of my *ravings*, of my fears, or of any terrible visions whatever; but *fancy* myself entirely composed, and that my *sleep, in particular*, is as sweet as that of a healthy, joyous little infant. I pray God that he will grant me a continuance of the same calm, but delightful, *dream*, until I come to know of those realities which "eyes have not seen, and which ears have not heard." I have scar[c]e realized that I am in prison, or in irons, at all. I certainly think I was never more cheerful in my life. I intend to take the liberty of sending, by express, to your care, some trifling articles for those of my family who may be in Ohio, which you can hand to my brother JEREMIAH, when you may see him, together with fifteen dollars I have asked him to advance to them. Please excuse me so often troubling you with my letters, or any of my matters. Please also remember me *most* kindly to MR. GRISWOLD, and to all others who love their neighbors. I write JEREMIAH to your care.

Your friend, in truth, John Brown.

———

Charlestown, Jefferson Co Va. 29th Nov. 1859

Mrs George L Stearns, Boston Mass

My Dear Friend

No letter I have received since my imprisonment here, has given me more satisfaction, or comfort; then yours on the 8th inst. I am quite cheerful; & was never more happy. Have only time [to] write you a word. May God forever reward you & *all yours. My love to all* who love their neighbors. I have asked to be *spared* from having any *mock; or hypocritical prayers made over me*, when I am publicly *murdered*: & that my only *religious attendants* be poor *little, dirty, ragged, bare headed, & barefooted Slave boys; & Girls*; led by some old *grey headed Slave Mother.*

Farewell. Farewell. Your Friend, John Brown.

———

Charlestown, Prison, Jefferson Co. Va. 30th Nov. 1859

My Dearly beloved Wife, Sons: & Daughters, *every one*

As I now begin what is probably the last letter I shall ever write to any of you; I conclude to write you all at the same time. I will mentions some little matters particularly applicable to little property concerns in another place. I yesterday received a letter from my wife from near Philadelphia: dated Nov 27th, by which it would seem that she has about given up the idea of seeing me again. I had written her to come on; if *she* felt equal to the undertaking; but I do not know as she will get my letter in time. It was on her *own account chiefly* that I asked her to stay *back* at first. I had a most strong desire to see her again; but there appeared to be very serious objections; & should we never meet in *this life*; I trust she will in the end be satisfied it was *for the best at least*; if not most for her comfort. I enclosed in my last letter to her a Draft of $50, Fifty Dollars from John Jay made payable to her order. I have now another to send her from my excellent old friend Edward Harris of Woonsocket Rhode Island for $100, One Hundred Dollars; which I shall *also make payable to her* order. I am writing the hour of my public *murder* with great composure of mind, & cheerfulness; feeling the strongest assurance that in no other possible way could I be used to so much advance the cause of God; & of humanity; & that nothing that either I or all my family have sacrificed or suffered: *will be lost*. The reflection that a *wise, & merciful, as well as Just, & holy God*: rules not only the affairs of *this world*; but of all worlds; is a rock to set our feet upon; under all circumstances; *even* those more severely *trying ones*: into which our own follies; & [w]rongs have placed us. I have now no doubt but that our seeming *disaster*: will ultimately result in the most *glorious success*. So my dear *shattered; & broken* family; be of good cheer; & believe & trust in God; "with all your heart; & with all your soul; for *he* doeth *All things well.*" Do not feel ashamed on my account; nor *for one moment* despair of the cause; or grow *weary* of *well doing*. I bless God; I never felt stronger confidence in the certain & near approach of a *bright Morning; & glorious day*; then I have felt; & do now feel; since my confinement here. I am endeavouring to "return" like a "poor Prodigal" *as I am*; to my Father: against whom I have *always* sined: *in the hope*; that he may kindly, & forgivingly "meet me: though; *a verry great way off.*" Oh my dear Wife & Children would "to God" you could know how I have been "traveling in birth for you" all; that no one of you "my fail of the grace of God, through Jesus Christ": that no one of you may be blind to the truth: & glorious "light of *his* word"; in which Life; & Immortality; are brought to light." I beseech you *every one* to make the bible your *dayly &*

Nightly study; with a *childlike honest, candid, teachable spirit*: out of love and respect for your Husband; & Father: & I beseech *the God* of *my Fathers*; to open all your eyes to a discovery of *the truth*. You *cannot imagine* how much *you* may *soon need* the consolations of the Christian religion.

Circumstances like my own; for more than a month past; convince me beyound *all doubt* of our great need: of something more to rest our hopes on; than merely our own vague theories framed up, while our *prejudices* are excited; *or* our *Vanity* worked up to its highest pitch. Oh do not trust your eternal all uppon the boisterous Ocean, without *even a Helm*; or *Compass* to *aid* you in steering. I do *not ask any* of you; to throw *away your reason*: I only *ask* you, to make a candid, & sober *use of your reason*: My dear younger children will you listen to this last poor admonition of one who can *only* love you? Oh be determined at once to give your whole hearts to God; & let *nothing shake*; *or alter*; that resolution. You need have no fear *of* REGRETING *it*. Do not be in vain; and thoughtless: but *sober minded*. And let me entreat you all to love *the whole remnant* or our once great family: "with a pure *heart fervently*." Try to *build again*: your broken walls: & to make *the utmost* of every *stone* that is left. Nothing can so tend to make life a blessing as the consciousness that you *love; & are beloved*: & "love ye the stranger" *still*. It is a ground of the utmost comfort to *my mind*: to know that so many of you as have had *the opportunity*; have given full proof of your fidelity to the great family of man. *Be faithful* until *death*. From the exercise of habitual love to man: *it cannot* be very *hard*: to *learn to love* his *maker*. I must *yet* insert a reason for my firm belief in the Divine inspiration of the Bible: notwithstanding I am (perhaps naturally) skeptical. (certainly not, *credulous*.) I wish you all to consider *it most thoroughly*; when you read that blessed book; & see whether you *can not* discover such evidence yourselves. It is the purity of *heart, feeling, or motive*: as well as *word, & action* which is every where insisted on; that distinguish it from *all other teachings*; that *commends it* to *my conscience*: whether *my heart* be "willing, & obedient" *or not*. The inducements that it holds out; are another reason *of my conviction* or its *truth: & genuineness*; that I cannot here *omit*; in this my *last argument*, for the Bible *Eternal life*: is that my soul *is "panting after" this moment*. I mention this; as reason for endeavouring to leave a valuable copy of the Bible to be carefully *preserved* in remembrance *of me*: to so many of my posterity; *instead* of some *other* thing: of equal *cost*. I beseech you all to live in habitual contentment with verry *moderate* circumstances: & gains, of *worldly store*: & most earnestly to teach this: to your *children;* & *Childrens, Children*; after you: by *example: as well*: as precept. Be determined to know by experience *as soon as may be*: whether bible instruction is of *Divine origin* or not; *which says;* "*Owe no man anything but* to love one another." John Rogers wrote to his children, "Abhor that arrant whore of Rome." John Brown writes to his children to abhor with *undiing hatred*, also: that "sum of all vilanies;" Slavery. *Remember* that "he that is *slow* to *anger* is *better* than the mighty: and he that ruleth his *spirit*; than he that taketh a city." Remember also: *that* "they that be *wise* shall *shine*: and they that *turn* many to *righteousness*: as the stars forever; & ever." And now dearly beloved *Farewell* To God & the word of his grace I comme[n]d you all.

Your Affectionate Husband & Father, John Brown

Charlestown, Va, 2d, December, 1859

I John Brown am now quite *certain* that the crimes of this *guilty land: will* never be purged *away*; but with Blood. I had as *I now think; vainly* flattered myself that without *verry much* bloodshed; it might be done.

4

Responses to John Brown's Raid

12

Northern and Southern Newspapers React to the Raid and Trial
1859

Newspapers across the nation reacted differently to Brown's raid and trial. For example, the Democratic New Hampshire Patriot *used the episode to tar "black republicans" who lauded Brown's earlier work in Kansas. In the South, the* Petersburg *(Virginia)* Express *argued that John Brown's raid was but one instance of a far-reaching Northern conspiracy designed to destroy slavery and the southern way of life. According to the editor of the* Charleston *(South Carolina)* Mercury, *a leading secessionist journal, "none can blind their eyes to the audacity of [Brown's] attempt, or fail to regard it as a pregnant sign of the times — a prelude to what must and will recur again and again, as the progress of sectional hate and Black Republican success advances to their consummation." The third editorial, from the Republican Albany, New York,* Evening Journal *urges Virginia Governor Wise to spare Brown's life and refers to his last speech at the trial as "sublime."*

12a. *New Hampshire Patriot*, October. 26, 1859; also available online at http://history .furman.edu/benson/docs/nhpajb59a26a.htm; 12b. *Petersburg* (Virginia) *Express*, reprinted in *Charleston Mercury*, October 25, 1859; 12c. Albany (New York) *Evening Journal*, November 30, 1859; also available online at http://history.furman.edu/benson/docs/nyajjb59b30a.htm.

NEW HAMPSHIRE PATRIOT
The Harpers Ferry Affair
October 26, 1859

The public mind throughout the country, during the past week, has been much agitated by the most deplorable events at Harpers Ferry, Va., an account of which we give in another part of this paper. The circumstances were of a nature to strongly attract public attention. A quiet community, in the night time, was startled by an insurrection in its very midst. The suddenness of the alarm, with the uncertainty of the nature and extent of the danger, at first paralyzed the people for any resistance, and the insurgents, being fully armed, gained possession of the place. But after a bloody conflict, resulting in the loss of twenty-one lives in all, the insurrection was quelled and order returned.

In this atrocious affair there were peculiar features to excite alarm, not only in the community where [it] occurred, but also throughout the country. Although the proposed object of it was the release of the slaves, yet it now clearly appears that they had no part in it. In fact, one of the first victims was a colored man, shot by the insurgents because he refused to join them. The chief actors, and by far the greater number, were white men. Neither was it a sudden outbreak, occasioned by some occurrence of the moment; but it was in pursuance of a plan deliberately considered and formed by men elsewhere, who had gone to that place for the very purpose of making preparations and carrying it into execution. These are the circumstances which render this insurrection of more than ordinary importance and deserving reflection.

Notwithstanding the melancholy result in the loss of so many lives, these events will not be without advantage to the country, if they shall serve to recall the public mind from prejudice and excitement to a clear and honest consideration of the dangerous tendencies of the pernicious doctrines which, during a few years past, have been so zealously taught and advocated by political leaders and partisan preachers here at the North. It is not a long time since not only on the stump, but even from the pulpit, "Sharpe's rifles" were recommended and applauded as the proper and best means for the relief of "bleeding Kansas." We then denounced those principles as deserving the severest condemnation, not more, certainly, on account of the circumstances of the particular case to which they were applied, than for their dangerous and fatal tendencies, if ever admitted as proper in practice. We could not admit violence or force as, in any case, a necessary or proper recourse, in this country, for the establishment of any political principles, or for relief from political evils. But we did not then expect so soon to see so striking a proof and illustration of the correctness of our views, as is now offered by these tragical events at Harpers Ferry. They are the natural and perfect fruit of the seed sown in Kansas. The instigator and leader at Harpers Ferry was Capt. John Brown of Kansas notoriety; his confederates here were his associates there, and the arms used were the very same "Sharpe's rifles" furnished for use in Kansas. It seems appropriate that it should have been so, and we may add, almost providential that these circumstances should thus concur to connect and identify the one transaction with the other. Gerrit Smith, in his letter to Brown enclosing funds to aid him in carrying into execution his nefarious schemes at Harpers Ferry, very truly and correctly calls it "Kansas work." It was, in principle, the same.

Those black republicans who have heretofore been so loud in their applause and instigation of the work of violence and bloodshed in Kansas, now seek to relieve themselves from the unfavorable consequences in the public mind of their recent "Kansas work" on another field, by stigmatizing Brown and his associates as fools and maniacs. It is true that extreme folly and madness are apparent in this Harpers Ferry affair; but that folly and madness were not so much error on their part with regard to the principle of the "Kansas work," as in the hopeless circumstances for success under which they undertook to carry it into practice. But in what position does this new view by these defenders of black republicanism, place that party? If Brown and his confederates were fools and madmen at Harpers Ferry, may they not have been such in Kansas also? And if so, who shall say how much of the wrong in that unfortunate territory is justly to be charged against those who were the instigators of these fools and madmen, and who placed in their hands the weapons for violence and bloodshed!

In the developments made by Brown and others since their capture, are many things for consideration. We have not time or room now to refer to them particularly. We hope the people of this State will carefully read the accounts of them for themselves. We wish, however, to call attention to the statement by Brown of his motives for going to

Kansas—that it was not for the purpose of making his home there, *but to take part in its troubles.* We all know how conspicuous and violent a part he took.—This shows how true is the charge, which has been so persistently denied by our opponents, that many of the misfortunes of that Territory have been owing to the interference and instigation of those abroad who really had no interest in or care for it, except so far as it could be used for political and partisan purposes.

Let us not be misunderstood. We do not intend to charge all the members of the black republican party as being responsible for this deplorable affair at Harpers Ferry. On the contrary, we know that most of them will denounce it in as strong terms as we do, and as it deserves. But we ask them to consider whether, if not the fair and natural consequence, it is not at least the probable effect of the principles and doctrine of arms and violence advocated by the black republican leaders for the relief of Kansas, and of the doctrine of "irrepressible conflict" which they are now urged to make the sum and substance of their political faith. For if such be their view of it, we know the people of this State will not support a party from whose principles or acts results so fatal, not only to the peace but even to the continuance of the Union, are in any degree likely to follow.

PETERSBURG (VIRGINIA) EXPRESS

The Harpers Ferry Conspiracy
October 25, 1859

The Insurrection

This Harpers Ferry affair is but a small eruption on the surface of a diseased body. Brown and his desperados are but a sign of the cancerous disease with which a great part of northern society is polluted by the traitorous views of men who have been raised to honor, and surrounded by applause, and maintained in power, by whole communities, and even whole States. What Seward teaches from New York State, Wilson and Sumner from Massachusetts, Fessenden from Maine, Chase from Ohio, Collamer from Vermont, Grow from Pennsylvania[1]—what

[1]Abolitionist U.S. senators.

public prints, that flourish too vigorously to be the mere propagandists of fanaticism supported by a small fraction of society—the *Tribunes*, and *Eras*, and the like—teach—all lead inevitably to collision as bitter as the late affair, but wide spread as the lines which divide southern institutions from northern. The Harpers Ferry affair was but premature fruit. A whole harvest of sterner rebellion and bloodier collision is growing up and ripening from the seed these men have sown.

Disguise it as we may, large portions of the North are our enemies—more bitter, more deadly hostile than though hereditary enmity had pitched their opposing hosts on a hundred battle-fields. The spirit of the effort to wrest Kansas from slavery, made by the concert of a party which polled more than a million votes at the last Presidential election, is manifest enough from the dead and captured agents of the bloody design at Harpers Ferry. Had one of the men of the irrepressible conflict school occupied the Presidency in the last five days, who can tell the bloody news which would, at this instant, be ringing through the land?

Unless a change—a speedy and effectual change—sweep over northern society, the great conflict must come.

Can we do more than hope that the change may come? Can we do less than prepare for its alternative? Shall we go to sleep with such a warning ringing in our ears?

The South has a work before her, which she must do, unless she is content to lie down in blindness and let an enemy steal away her strength. We can force northern communities to cultivate fraternity, and to clear themselves of the pollution in their midst. We can cut off, by our own voluntary act, the trade which makes them prosperous, and build up our own energies at home. And we can arm—aye, arm!

If our young men will do their duty, we shall see, instead of three companies with meagre ranks, in this city, and a few here and there scattered in the country around, whole regiments spring up. Every militiaman should be armed and drilled. The very smallest sacrifice of time or money on the part of our people is requisite to give us men enough for any emergency, as ready for work as the gallant volunteers which sprang to the call of the Governor in the late danger. No one knows how soon this may be necessary, but all can see that preparation may be the only security.

ALBANY, NEW YORK, EVENING JOURNAL

From the Philadelphia Press
November 30, 1859

"We do not believe there is any purpose, such as the Enquirer inti-
mates, to attempt the rescue of John Brown on the 2d of December.
We do not believe that any body of men would make such an experiment, especially in view of the somewhat formidable preparations of
the military of the gallant State. John Brown will meet his fate,
whether as a bad man or as a madman, with comparative little sympathy. Our own belief is that he should not be executed; but if the seeds
of future excitement are planted on his tomb, we do not doubt it will
be found that they were placed there as well by his Southern enemies
as by his Northern sympathisers."

Whatever of sympathy the fate of John Brown awakens, will be
occasioned by his bearing through an ordeal so trying, rather than
any complicity of feeling in his lawless enterprise. Upon the question
whether he had any right to go there with such intentions, or whether,
when taken, he ought to be punished, there is no general difference of
opinion or sentiment. Though we "would that all men" were Free, we
should as readily go to Virginia to run off their Horses and Cattle, as
their Slaves. By the Constitution and Laws, Slavery is recognized and
tolerated. It was a compact made by our Fathers, and one that binds
their heirs. We will oppose both its extension and its encroachments.
Thus far, and no farther, goes our sense of duty to Freedom.

John Brown seems to have counted the cost of his enterprise; and,
like a brave man, is prepared to meet his fate. Since the day that Paul
spoke to Agrippa,[1] we have read nothing more truly sublime than
John Brown's response to the Tribunal before which he stood to
receive Sentence of Death.

The "pomp and circumstance of War" with which the execution
of Brown is to be surrounded, was wholly unnecessary. The rescue
rumors were entirely unfounded. All this display of Troops is for
effect. Gov. Wise intends to make what capital can be made out of this
Execution.

---

[1]A biblical reference to Acts 25:13–26:32, in which the apostle Paul advocates Christianity to King Agrippa II.

We agree with the *"Press"* in the opinion that in this case *forbearance* would be *wisdom,* though neither John Brown or his Family ask it. But Gov. Wise is entitled to and means to insist upon all that is "nominated in the bond." And John Brown, imbued with the conviction that "hanging is the best use" that can be made of him, calmly awaits his day and hour of doom.

<h1 style="text-align:center">13</h1>

HENRY DAVID THOREAU

A Plea for Captain John Brown

October 30, 1859

Henry David Thoreau—author, political activist, and one of the foremost members of the Transcendentalist philosophical movement, which emphasized individualism and critical thought—shared with John Brown a hatred of slavery and of the federal government's defense of it. In response to the U.S. war with Mexico and Southern demands for a federal fugitive slave law, Thoreau wrote an essay entitled Resistance to Civil Government, *better known as "Civil Disobedience." The 1849 essay lays out Thoreau's belief that citizens' consciences must occasionally overrule unjust laws and that individuals have a duty to avoid being made agents of injustice by their leaders. Thoreau famously went to jail rather than pay taxes to a government that he argued would help fund federal slave catchers under the new Fugitive Slave Law.*

In his speech "A Plea for Captain John Brown," first delivered in Thoreau's hometown of Concord, Massachusetts, just two weeks after the raid on Harpers Ferry, Thoreau offered the first full-throated defense of Brown's actions. This placed him squarely against popular opinion of the time, which held that Brown's actions were foolish and that he was likely insane; even the abolitionist Liberator *called the raid a "misguided, wild, and apparently insane effort." On the contrary, Thoreau argued,*

James Redpath, *Echoes of Harper's Ferry* (Boston: Thayer and Eldridge, 1860), 17–42.

Brown's commitment to justice and equality forced *him to battle state-sponsored injustice. Far from being a horse thief and a murderer, Thoreau praised Brown as thoughtful, moral, and humane. "I plead not for his life, but for his character—his immortal life," he said. "He is not Brown any longer; he is an angel of light."*

I trust that you will pardon me for being here. I do not wish to force my thoughts upon you, but I feel forced myself. Little as I know of Captain Brown, I would fain[1] do my part to correct the tone and the statements of the newspapers, and of my countrymen generally, respecting his character and actions. It costs us nothing to be just. We can at least express our sympathy with, and admiration of, him and his companions, and that is what I now propose to do. . . .

He was by descent and birth a New England farmer, a man of great common sense, deliberate and practical as that class is, and tenfold more so. He was like the best of those who stood at Concord Bridge once, on Lexington Common, and on Bunker Hill, only he was firmer and higher principled than any that I have chanced to hear of as there. It was no abolition lecturer that converted him. Ethan Allen and Stark,[2] with whom he may in some respects be compared, were rangers in lower and less important fields. They could bravely face their country's foes, but he had the courage to face his country herself, when she was in the wrong. A Western writer says, to account for his escape from so many perils, that he was conceived under a "rural exterior"; as if, in that prairie land, a hero should, by good rights, wear a citizen's dress only.

He did not go to the college called Harvard, good old Alma Mater as she is. He was not fed on the pap that is there furnished. As he phrased it, "I know no more of grammar than one of your calves." But he went to the great University of the West, where he sedulously pursued the study of Liberty, for which he had early betrayed a fondness, and having taken many degrees, he finally commenced the public practice of Humanity in Kansas, as you all know. Such were *his humanities*, and not any study of grammar. He would have left a Greek accent slanting the wrong way, and righted up a falling man.

[1] Gladly.
[2] Ethan Allen and John Stark were both Revolutionary War heroes.

He was one of that class of whom we hear a great deal, but, for the most part, see nothing at all—the Puritans. It would be in vain to kill him. He died lately in the time of Cromwell,[3] but he reappeared here. Why should he not? Some of the Puritan stock are said to have come over and settled in New England. They were a class that did something else than celebrate their forefathers' day, and eat parched corn in remembrance of that time. They were neither Democrats nor Republicans, but men of simple habits, straightforward, prayerful; not thinking much of rulers who did not fear God, not making many compromises, nor seeking after available candidates.

"In his camp," as one has recently written, and as I have myself heard him state, "he permitted no profanity; no man of loose morals was suffered to remain there, unless, indeed, as a prisoner of war. 'I would rather,' said he, 'have the small-pox, yellow fever, and cholera, all together in my camp, than a man without principle. . . . It is a mistake, sir, that our people make, when they think that bullies are the best fighters, or that they are the fit men to oppose these Southerners. Give me men of good principles—Godfearing men—men who respect themselves, and with a dozen of them I will oppose any hundred such men as these Buford ruffians.' " He said that if one offered himself to be a soldier under him, who was forward to tell what he could or would do, if he could only get sight of the enemy, he had but little confidence in him.

He was never able to find more than a score or so of recruits whom he would accept, and only about a dozen, among them his sons, in whom he had perfect faith. When he was here, some years ago, he showed to a few a little manuscript book—his "orderly book" I think he called it—containing the names of his company in Kansas, and the rules by which they bound themselves; and he stated that several of them had already sealed the contract with their blood. When some one remarked that, with the addition of a chaplain, it would have been a perfect Cromwellian troop, he observed that he would have been glad to add a chaplain to the list, if he could have found one that would fill that office worthily. It is easy enough to find one for the United States army. I believe that he had prayers in his camp morning and evening, nevertheless.

He was a man of Spartan habits, and at sixty was scrupulous about his diet at your table, excusing himself by saying that he must eat

---

[3]Oliver Cromwell, Lord Protector of Britain from 1653 to 1658.

sparingly and fare hard, as became a soldier or one who was fitting himself for difficult enterprises, a life of exposure.

A man of rare common sense and directness of speech, as of action; a transcendentalist above all, a man of ideas and principles—that was what distinguished him. Not yielding to a whim or transient impulse, but carrying out the purpose of a life. I noticed that he did not over-state anything, but spoke within bounds. I remember, particularly, how, in his speech here, he referred to what his family had suffered in Kansas, without ever giving the least vent to his pent-up fire. It was a volcano with an ordinary chimney-flue. Also referring to the deeds of certain Border Ruffians,[4] he said, rapidly paring away his speech, like an experienced soldier, keeping a reserve of force and meaning, "They had a perfect right to be hung." He was not in the least a rhetorician, was not talking to Buncombe or his constituents any-where, had no need to invent anything, but to tell the simple truth, and communicate his own resolution; therefore he appeared incompa-rably strong, and eloquence in Congress and elsewhere seemed to me at a discount. It was like the speeches of Cromwell compared with those of an ordinary king.

As for his tact and prudence, I will merely say, that at a time when scarcely a man from the Free States was able to reach Kansas by any direct route, at least without having his arms taken from him, he, car-rying what imperfect guns and other weapons he could collect, openly and slowly drove an ox-cart through Missouri, apparently in the capac-ity of a surveyor, with his surveying compass exposed in it, and so passed unsuspected, and had ample opportunity to learn the designs of the enemy. For some time after his arrival he still followed the same profession. When, for instance, he saw a knot of ruffians on the prairie, discussing, of course, the single topic which then occupied their minds, he would, perhaps, take his compass and one of his sons, and proceed to run an imaginary line right through the very spot on which that conclave had assembled, and when he came up to them, he would naturally pause and have some talk with them, learning their news, and, at last, all their plans perfectly; and having thus completed his real survey, he would resume his imaginary one, and run on his line till he was out of sight.

When I expressed a surprise that he could live in Kansas at all, with a price set upon his head, and so large a number, including the authorities,

---

[4]Proslavery activists who moved to Kansas from neighboring slave states.

exasperated against him, he accounted for it by saying, "It is perfectly well understood that I will not be taken." Much of the time for some years he had to skulk in swamps, suffering from poverty and from sickness, which was the consequence of exposure, befriended only by Indians and a few whites. But though it might be known that he was lurking in a particular swamp, his foes commonly did not care to go in after him. He could even come out into a town where there were more Border Ruffians than Free State men, and transact some business, without delaying long, and yet not be molested; for said he, "No little handful of men were willing to undertake it, and a large body could not be got together in season."

As for his recent failure, we do not know the facts about it. It was evidently far from being a wild and desperate attempt. His enemy, Mr. Vallandigham, is compelled to say, that "it was among the best planned and executed conspiracies that ever failed."

Not to mention his other successes, was it a failure, or did it show a want of good management, to deliver from bondage a dozen human beings, and walk off with them by broad daylight, for weeks if not months, at a leisurely pace, through one State after another, for half the length of the North, conspicuous to all parties, with a price set upon his head, going into a courtroom on his way and telling what he had done, thus convincing Missouri that it was not profitable to try to hold slaves in his neighborhood?—and this, not because the government menials were lenient, but because they were afraid of him.

Yet he did not attribute his success, foolishly, to "his star," or to any magic. He said, truly, that the reason why such greatly superior numbers quailed before him, was, as one of his prisoners confessed, because they *lacked a cause*—a kind of armor which he and his party never lacked. When the time came, few men were found willing to lay down their lives in defense of what they knew to be wrong; they did not like that this should be their last act in this world.

But to make haste to *his* last act, and its effects.

The newspapers seem to ignore, or are perhaps really ignorant of the fact, that there are at least as many as two or three individuals to a town throughout the North who think much as the present speaker does about him and his enterprise. I do not hesitate to say that they are an important and growing party. We aspire to be something more than stupid and timid chattels, pretending to read history and our Bibles, but desecrating every house and every day we breathe in. Perhaps anxious politicians may prove that only seventeen white men and five Negroes were concerned in the late enterprise; but their very anxiety to prove this might suggest to themselves that all is not told. Why do they still dodge the truth? They are so anxious because of a dim consciousness of the fact, which they do not distinctly face, that at least a million of the free inhabitants of the United States would have rejoiced if it had succeeded. They at most only criticise the tactics. Though we wear no crape,[5] the thought of that man's position and probable fate is spoiling many a man's day here at the North for other thinking. If anyone who has seen him here can pursue successfully any other train of thought, I do not know what he is made of. If there is any such who gets his usual allowance of sleep, I will warrant him to fatten easily under any circumstances which do not touch his body or purse. I put a piece of paper and a pencil under my pillow, and when I could not sleep, I wrote in the dark. . . .

I read all the newspapers I could get within a week after this event, and I do not remember in them a single expression of sympathy for these men. I have since seen one noble statement, in a Boston paper, not editorial. Some voluminous sheets decided not to print the full report of Brown's words to the exclusion of other matter. It was as if the publisher should reject the manuscript of the New Testament, and print Wilson's[6] last speech. The same journal which contained this pregnant news, was chiefly filled, in parallel columns, with the reports of the political conventions that were being held. But the descent to them was too steep. They should have been spared this contrast, been printed in an extra at least. To turn from the voices and deeds of earnest men to the cackling of political conventions! Office-seekers and speech-makers, who do not so much as lay an honest egg, but wear their breasts bare upon an egg of chalk! Their great game is the game of straws, or rather that universal aboriginal game of the platter, at which the Indians cried *hub, bub!* Exclude the reports of religious and political conventions, and publish the words of a living man.

But I object not so much to what they have omitted, as to what they have inserted. Even the *Liberator* called it "a misguided, wild, and apparently insane effort." As for the herd of newspapers and magazines, I do not chance to know an editor in the country who will deliberately print any thing which he knows will ultimately and permanently reduce the number of his subscribers. They do not believe that it

---

[5]A fabric traditionally worn to signify mourning.
[6]Henry Wilson, the "Natick Cobbler," was a U.S. senator from Massachusetts and, later, vice president of the United States.

would be expedient. How then can they print truth? If we do not say pleasant things, they argue, nobody will attend to us. And so they do like some traveling auctioneers, who sing an obscene song in order to draw a crowd around them. Republican editors, obliged to get their sentences ready for the morning edition, and accustomed to look at everything by the twilight of politics, express no admiration, nor true sorrow even, but call these men "deluded fanatics"—"mistaken men"—"insane," or "crazed." It suggests what a *sane* set of editors we are Blessed with, *not* "mistaken men"; who know very well on which side their bread is buttered, at least.

A man does a brave and humane deed, and at once, on all sides, we hear people and parties declaring, "I didn't do it, nor countenance *him* to do it, in any conceivable way. It can't be fairly inferred from my past career." I, for one, am not interested to hear you define your position. I don't know that I ever was, or ever shall be. I think it is mere egotism, or impertinent at this time. Ye needn't take so much pains to wash your skirts of him. No intelligent man will ever be convinced that he was any creature of yours. He went and came, as he himself informs us, "under the auspices of John Brown and nobody else." The Republican party does not perceive how many his failure will make to vote more correctly than they would have them. They have counted the votes of Pennsylvania and Co., but they have not correctly counted Captain Brown's votes. He has taken the wind out of their sails, the little wind they had, and they may as well lie to and repair.

What though he did not belong to your clique! Though you may not approve of his method or his principles, recognize his magnanimity. Would you not like to claim kindredship with him in that, though in no other thing he is like, or likely, to you? Do you think that you would lose your reputation so? What you lost at the spile, you would gain at the bung.

If they do not mean all this, then they do not speak the truth, and say what they mean. They are simply at their old tricks still.

"It was always conceded to him," *says one who calls him crazy*, "that he was a conscientious man, very modest in his demeanor, apparently inoffensive, until the subject of Slavery was introduced, when he would exhibit a feeling of indignation unparalleled."

The slave-ship is on her way, crowded with its dying victims; new cargoes are being added in mid ocean; a small crew of slaveholders, countenanced by a large body of passengers, is smothering four million under the hatches, and yet the politician asserts that the only proper way by which deliverance is to be obtained, is by "the quiet diffusion of the sentiments of humanity," without any "outbreak." As if the sentiments of humanity were ever found unaccompanied by its deeds, and you could disperse them, all finished to order, the pure article, as easily as water with a watering-pot, and so lay the dust. What is that that I hear cast overboard? The bodies of the dead that have found deliverence. That is the way we are "diffusing" humanity, and its sentiments with it.

Prominent and influential editors, accustomed to deal with politicians, men of an infinitely lower grade, say, in their ignorance, that he acted "on the principle of revenge." They do not know the man. They must enlarge themselves to conceive of him. I have no doubt that the time will come when they will begin to see him as he was. They have got to conceive of a man of faith and of religious principle, and not a politician nor an Indian; of a man who did not wait until he was personally interfered with or thwarted in some harmless business before he gave his life to the cause of the oppressed.

If Walker[7] may be considered the representative of the South, I wish I could say that Brown was the representative of the North. He was a superior man. He did not value his bodily life in comparison with ideal things. He did not recognize unjust human laws, but resisted them as he was bid. For once we are lifted out of the trivialness and dust of politics into the region of truth and manhood. No man in America has ever stood up so persistently or effectively for the dignity of human nature, knowing himself for a man, and the equal of any and all governments. In that sense he was the most American of us all. He needed no babbling lawyer, making false issues, to defend him. He was more than a match for all the judges that American voters, or officeholders of whatever grade, can create. He could not have been tried by a jury of his peers, because his peers did not exist. When a man stands up serenely against the condemnation and vengeance of mankind, rising above them literally *by a whole body*—even though he were of late the vilest murderer, who has settled that matter with himself—the spectacle is a sublime one—didn't ye know it, ye Liberators, ye Tribunes, ye Republicans?—and we become criminal in comparison. Do yourselves the honor to recognize him. He needs none of your respect.

---

[7]The American journalist William Walker took over the government of Nicaragua in 1855 and was recognized as president by Franklin Pierce. Walker was forced to return to the United States in 1857, but he later returned to Central America and was executed in Honduras in 1860.

As for the Democratic journals, they are not human enough to affect me at all. I do not feel indignation at anything they may say.

I am aware that I anticipate a little, that he was still, at the last accounts, alive in the hands of his foes; but that being the case, I have all along found myself thinking and speaking of him as physically dead.

I do not believe in erecting statues to those who still live in our hearts, whose bones have not yet crumbled in the earth around us, but I would rather see the statue of Captain Brown in the Massachusetts State-House yard, than that of any other man whom I know. I rejoice that I live in this age—that I am his contemporary.

What a contrast, when we turn to that political party which is so anxiously shuffling him and his plot out of its way, and looking around for some available slaveholder, perhaps, to be its candidate, at least for one who will execute the Fugitive Slave Law, and all those other unjust laws which he took up arms to annul!

Insane! A father and six sons, and one son-in-law, and several more men besides—as many at least as twelve disciples—all struck with insanity at once; while the sane tyrant holds with a firmer grip than ever his four millions of slaves, and a thousand sane editors, his abettors, are saving their country and their bacon! Just as insane were his efforts in Kansas. Ask the tyrant who is his most dangerous foe, the sane man or the insane. Do the thousands who know him best, who have rejoiced at his deeds in Kansas, and have afforded him material aid there, think him insane? Such a use of this word is a mere trope with most who persist in using it, and I have no doubt that many of the rest have already in silence retracted their words.

Read his admirable answers to Mason and others. How they are dwarfed and defeated by the contrast! On the one side, half brutish, half timid questioning; on the other, truth, clear as lightning, crashing into their obscene temples. They are made to stand with Pilate, and Gessler, and the Inquisition. How ineffectual their speech and action! and what a void their silence! They are but helpless tools in this great work. It was no human power that gathered them about this preacher.

What have Massachusetts and the North sent a few *sane* representatives to Congress for, of late years?—to declare with effect what kind of sentiments? All their speeches put together and boiled down, and probably they themselves will confess it, do not match for manly directness and force, and for simple truth, the few casual remarks of crazy John Brown, on the floor of the Harpers Ferry engine house; that man whom you are about to hang, to send to the other world, though not to represent *you* there. No, he was not our representative in any sense. He was too fair a specimen of a man to represent the likes of us. Who, then, *were* his constituents? If you read his words understandingly you will find out. In his case there is no idle eloquence, no made, nor maiden, speech, no compliments to the oppressor. Truth is his inspirer, and earnestness the polisher of his sentences. He could afford to lose his Sharpe's rifles, while he retained his faculty of speech, a Sharpe's rifle of infinitely surer and longer range.

And the *New York Herald* reports the conversation "verbatim"! It does not know of what undying words it is made the vehicle.

I have no respect for the penetration of any man who can read the report of that conversation, and still call the principal in it insane. It has the ring of a saner sanity than an ordinary discipline and habits of life, than an ordinary organization, secure. Take any sentence of it— "Any questions that I can honorably answer, I will; not otherwise. So far as I am myself concerned, I have told everything truthfully. I value my word, sir." The few who talk about his vindictive spirit, while they really admire his heroism, have no test by which to detect a noble man, no amalgam to combine with his pure gold. They mix their own dross with it.

It is relief to turn from these slanders to the testimony of his more truthful, but frightened, jailers and hangmen. Governor Wise speaks far more justly and appreciatingly of him than any Northern editor, or politician, or public personage, that I chance to have heard from. I know that you can afford to hear him again on this subject. He says: "They are themselves mistaken who take him to be a madman. . . . He is cool, collected, and indomitable, and it is but just to him to say, that he was humane to his prisoners. . . . And he inspired me with great trust in his integrity as a man of truth. He is a fanatic, vain and garrulous" (I leave that part to Mr. Wise) "firm, truthful, and intelligent. His men, too, who survive, are like him. . . . Colonel Washington says that he was the coolest and firmest man he ever saw in defying danger and death. With one son dead by his side, and another shot through, he felt the pulse of his dying son with one hand, and held his rifle with the other, and commanded his men with the utmost composure, encouraging them to be firm, and to sell their lives as dear as they could. Of the three white prisoners, Brown, Stephens, and Coppic, it was hard to say which was most firm."

Almost the first Northern men whom the slaveholder has learned to respect!

The testimony of Mr. Vallandigham, though less valuable, is of the same purport, that "it is vain to underrate either the man or his conspiracy. . . . He is the farthest possible remove from the ordinary ruffian, fanatic, or madman."

"All is quiet at Harpers Ferry," says the journals. What is the character of that calm which follows when the law and the slaveholder prevail? I regard this event as a touchstone designed to bring out, with glaring distinctness, the character of this government. We needed to be thus assisted to see it by the light of history. It needed to see itself. When a government puts forth its strength on the side of injustice, as ours to maintain Slavery and kill the liberators of the slave, it reveals itself a merely brute force, or worse, a demoniacal force. It is the head of the Plug Uglies. It is more manifest than ever that tyranny rules. I see this government to be effectually allied with France and Austria in oppressing mankind. There sits a tyrant holding fettered four millions of slaves; here comes their heroic liberator. This most hypocritical and diabolical government looks up from its seat on the gasping four millions, and inquires with an assumption of innocence, "What do you assault me for? Am I not an honest man? Cease agitation on this subject, or I will make a slave of you, too, or else hang you." . . .

This event advertises me that there is such a fact as death—the possibility of a man's dying. It seems as if no man had ever died in America before, for in order to die you must first have lived. I don't believe in the hearses, and palls, and funerals that they have had. There was no death in the case, because there had been no life; they merely rotted or sloughed off, pretty much as they had rotted or sloughed along. No temple's vail was rent, only a hole dug somewhere. Let the dead bury their dead. The best of them fairly ran down like a clock. Franklin—Washington—they were let off without dying; they were merely missing one day. I hear a good many pretend that they are going to die; or that they have died, for aught that I know. Nonsense! I'll defy them to do it. They haven't got life enough in them. They'll deliquesce like fungi, and keep a hundred eulogists mopping the spot where they left off. Only half a dozen or so have died since the world began. Do you think that you are going to die, sir? No! there's no hope of you. You haven't got your lesson yet. You've got to stay after school. We make a needless ado about capital punishment—taking lives, when there is no life to take. *Memento mori!*[8]

---

[8]A Latin motto meaning "Remember that you will die."

We don't understand that sublime sentence which some worthy got sculptured on his gravestone once. We've interpreted it in a grovelling and snivelling sense; we've wholly forgotten how to die. . . .

But be sure to die, nevertheless. Do your work, and finish it. If you know how to begin, you will know when to end.

These men, in teaching us how to die, have at the same time taught us how to live. If this man's acts and words do not create a revival, it will be the severest possible satire on the acts and words that do. It is the best news that America has ever heard. It has already quickened the feeble pulse of the North, and infused more and more generous blood into her veins and heart, than any number of years of what is called commercial and political prosperity could. How many a man who was lately contemplating suicide has now something to live for! . . .

I am here to plead his cause with you. I plead not for his life, but for his character—his immortal life; and so it becomes your cause wholly, and is not his in the least. Some eighteen hundred years ago Christ was crucified; this morning, perchance, Captain Brown was hung. These are the two ends of a chain which is not without its links. He is not Old Brown any longer; he is an angel of light.

I see now that it was necessary that the bravest and humanest man in all the country should be hung. Perhaps he saw it himself. I *almost fear* that I may yet hear of his deliverance, doubting if a prolonged life, if *any* life, can do as much good as his death.

"Misguided"! "Garrulous"! "Insane"! "Vindictive"! So ye write in your easy chairs, and thus he wounded responds from the floor of the Armory, clear as a cloudless sky, true as the voice of nature is: "No man sent me here; it was my own prompting and that of my Maker. I acknowledge no master in human form."

And in what a sweet and noble strain he proceeds, addressing his captors, who stand over him: "I think, my friends, you are guilty of a great wrong against God and humanity, and it would be perfectly right for any one to interfere with you so far as to free those you wilfully and wickedly hold in bondage." . . .

I foresee the time when the painter will paint that scene, no longer going to Rome for a subject; the poet will sing it; the historian record it; and, with the Landing of the Pilgrims and the Declaration of Independence, it will be the ornament of some future national gallery, when at least the present form of Slavery shall be no more here. We shall then be at liberty to weep for Captain Brown. Then, and not till then, we will take our revenge.

GOVERNOR HENRY WISE

Message to the Virginia Legislature

December 5, 1859

Governor Henry A. Wise of Virginia was among the first officeholders to arrive at Harpers Ferry after John Brown's capture. A former congressman with presidential ambitions, Wise had worked hard to develop relationships with Northern Democrats, but his political future would forever be linked with John Brown. Unlike many of his fellow Southerners, Wise developed a deep respect for his foe, saying he "inspired me with great trust in his integrity as a man of truth . . . [he is] the gamest man I ever saw." After the trial Wise had to struggle with determining Brown's fate: Should he go against his firsthand observations and declare Brown insane, commute Brown's sentence to life in prison and risk enflaming the South, or go forward with the execution and make Brown a martyr?

With popular opinion what it was in the South, Wise had no real choice but to execute Brown for his crimes. In his message to the Virginia Legislature three days after Brown was hanged, Wise justified his decision, although he was well aware that doing so could unify the North and strengthen secessionists in his own state and section.

Gentlemen: Up to a late period I had fondly hoped to close my official term and part from my executive labors with naught but cause of congratulation on the condition of the commonwealth. But, the uppermost theme in this my last regular message must be that our peace has been disturbed; our citizens have been imprisoned, robbed and murdered; the sanctity of their dwellings has been violated; their persons have been outraged; their property has been seized by force of arms; a stronghold in their midst, with its arms and munitions of war, has been captured, and the inhabitants cut off from the means of defense; a national highway through our limits, and its locomotive trains and telegraphic wires have been stopped; the state and national sovereignties have been insulted and assailed; and state and federal troops have

---

New York Times, December 5, 1859, p. 1.

been called out and been compelled to fight, at the loss of several, killed and wounded, to subdue rebellion and treason, at Harpers Ferry in the county of Jefferson, within our jurisdiction.

This was no result of ordinary crimes, however highhanded and felonious. It was no conspiracy of bandits against society in general, with the motives which usually actuate criminals, confined to the individual perpetrators, and to be crushed by their arrest and punishment. But it was an extraordinary and actual invasion, by a sectional organization, specially upon slaveholders and upon their property in Negro slaves. The home to be invaded was the home of domestic slavery; the persons to be seized were the persons of slaveholders; the property to be confiscated was the property in slaves and the other property of slaveholders alone, such as money, plate, jewels and other of like kind, which was to be taken to compensate the robbers for the trouble and risk of robbing the masters of their slaves; the slaves were not to be taken to be carried away, but they were to be made to stand by the side of the robbers, and to be forced to fight to liberate themselves by massacreing their masters; the arsenal was taken to supply arms to servile insurgents; and a provisional government was attempted, in a British province, by our own countrymen, united to us in the faith of confederacy, combining with Canadians, to invade the slaveholding states of the United States; and thus the night of the 16th of October last was surprised and the day of the 17th of October last was startled by the signal guns of rapine, murder, robbery and treason, begun at Harpers Ferry for the purpose of stirring up universal insurrection of slaves throughout the whole South.

Sudden, surprising, shocking as this invasion has been, it is not more so than the rapidity and rancor of the causes which have prompted and put it in motion. It is not confined to the parties who were the present participators in its outrages. Causes and influences lie behind it more potent [by] far than the little band of desperadoes who were sent ahead to kindle the sparks of a general conflagration; and the event, sad as it is, would deserve but little comment, if the condign punishment of the immediate perpetrators of the felonies committed would for the future secure the peace which has been disturbed, and guarantee the safety which is threatened. Indeed, if the miserable convicts were the only conspirators against our peace and safety, we might have forgiven their offenses and constrained them only by the grace of pardon. But an entire social and sectional sympathy has incited their crimes, and now rises in rebellion and insurrection to the height of sustaining and justifying their enormity.

It would be pusillanimous to shut our eyes and to affect not to see certain facts of fearful import which stare us in the face, and of which I must speak plainly to you, with the firm and manly purpose of meeting danger and with no weak and wicked design of exciting agitation. That danger exists, of serious magnitude, there can be no doubt in the minds of the most calm and reflecting, and the way to avert it in all cases is to march up to it and meet it front to front. If it has not grown too great already, it will retire from collision; and if it has grown strong enough already for the encounter, it had better be met at once for it will not diminish by delay. I believe in truth, that the very policy of the prime promoters of this apparently mad movement is purely tentative: to try whether we will face the danger which is now sealed in blood. If we "take the dare," the aggression will become more and more insolent; and, if we do not, it will either truckle or meet us in open conflict to be subdued; and, in either event, our safety and the national peace will be best secured by a direct settlement at once— the sooner the better.

For a series of years social and sectional differences have been growing up, unhappily, between the states of our Union and their people. An evil spirit of fanaticism has seized upon negro slavery as the one object of social reform, and the one idea of its abolition has seemed to madden whole masses of one entire section of the country. It enters into their religion, into their education, into their politics and prayers, into their courts of justice, into their business, into their legislatures, into all classes of their people, the most respectable and most lawful, into their pulpits and into their presses and school-houses, into their men, women and children of all ages, everywhere. It has trained three generations, from childhood up, in moral and social habits of hatred to masters of African slaves in the United States. It turns not upon slavery elsewhere, or against slaveholders in any other country, but is especially malignant and vindictive towards its own countrymen, for the very reason that it is bound to them by the faith and sanction of a confederate law. To set up that law to it is to enrage it by the sight of the law, because it is bound by it. It has been taught by the Atheism of a "higher law" than that of a regular government bound by constitutions and statutes. It has been made to believe in the doctrine of absolute individual rights, independent of all relations of man to man in a conventional and social form; and that each man for himself has the prerogative to set up his conscience, his will and his judgment over and above all legal enactments and social institutions. It has been enflamed by prostituted teachers and preachers and presses to do and dare any crime and its consequences which may set up its individual supremacy over law and order. It has been taught from the senate chamber to trust in the fatality of an "irrepressible conflict," into which it is bound to plunge. Its anti-Christ pulpit has breathed naught but insurrectionary wrath into servants against their masters, and has denounced our national union as a covenant with death for recognizing property in slaves and guaranteeing to it the protection of law. It has raised contributions in churches to furnish arms and money to such criminals as these to make a war for empire of settlement in our new territories. It has trained them on the frontier and there taught them the skill of the Indian in savage warfare, and then turned them back upon the oldest and largest slave-holding state to surprise one of its strongest holds. It has organized in Canada and traversed and corresponded thence to New Orleans and from Boston to Iowa. It has established spies everywhere, and has secret agents in the heart of every slave state, and has secret associations and "underground railroads" in every free state. It enlists influence and money at home and abroad. It has sent comforters and counsellors and sympathy, and would have sent rescue to these assassins, robbers, murderers and traitors, whom it sent to felons' graves. It has openly and secretly threatened vengeance on the execution of our laws. And since their violation it has defiantly proclaimed aloud that "insurrection is the lesson of the hour"—not of slaves only, but all are to be free to rise up against fixed government, and no government is to be allowed except "the average common sense of the masses," and no protection is to be permitted against that power.

This is but an epitome, plain and unvarnished, without exaggeration. What is this but anarchy? What does it mean but "confusion worse confounded," and the overthrow of all rights, of all property, of all government, of all religion, of all rule among men? Nothing but mad riot can rule and misrule with such sentiments as these. There can be no compromise with them, no toleration of them in safety or with self-respect. They must be met and crushed, or they will crush us, or our union with non-slaveholding states cannot continue.

The strongest argument against this unnatural war upon negro slavery in one section by another of the same common country, is that it inevitably drives to disunion of the states, embittered with all the vengeful hate of civil war. As that union is among the most precious of our blessings, so the argument ought to weigh which weighs its value. But this consideration is despised by fanaticism. It contemns the Union, and now contemns us for clinging to it as we do. It scoffs the warning that the Union is endangered. The Union itself is denounced as a covenant with sin, and we are scorned as too timid to make the warning of danger to it worthy to be heeded. It arrogantly assumes to break all the bonds of faith within it, and defies the attempt to escape oppression without it. *This rudely assails our honor* as well as our interest, and demands of us what we will do. We have but one thing to do; unless the numerical majority will cease to violate confederate faith, on a question of such vital importance to us, and will cease, immediately and absolutely cease to disturb our peace, to destroy our lives and property, and to deprive us of all protection and redress under the perverted forms and distorted workings of the Union, we must take up arms. The issue is too essential to be compromised any more. We cannot stand such insults and outrages as those of Harpers Ferry without suffering worse than the death of citizens: without suffering dishonor, the death of a state. . . .

Never were prisoners treated with more lenity of trial. And never in any case, in the history of trials, was justice administered with more forbearance, more calmness, more dignity and more majesty of law — never were such prisoners treated with as much benignant kindness as they have been by the people whom they outraged sufficiently to have incited summary punishment.

To prevent any such punishment on the one hand, and a rescue on the other; to guard justice, in a word, I called into service military guards, to aid the civil authority and keep the peace. Receiving information that organization of guards was necessary, I sent an aid to the scene, there to see what was wanting, to assist the adjutant general, and to pass my orders. Col. J. Lucius Davis, a competent soldier, volunteered his services, and I accepted them, to organize the corps, to distribute arms, to post guards and to provide subsistence and quarters, and to call for whatever was wanting. These services he continued most faithfully and efficiently to perform, with my full approbation, until very recent events made it necessary to call for more troops; and Major General William B. Taliaferro, of the fourth division, repaired to the place, and volunteered in person to take command. Many of the troops were from his division, and I could not decline the tender of his services. During the trial of the prisoners and since, appeals and threats of every sort, the most extraordinary, from every quarter, have been made to the executive. I lay before you the mass of these, it being impossible to enter into their details. Though the laws do not permit me to pardon in cases of treason, yet pardons and reprieves have been demanded on the grounds of, 1st, insanity; 2nd, magnanimity; 3d, the policy of not making martyrs.

As to the first, the parties by themselves or counsel put in no plea of insanity. No insanity was feigned even; the prisoner Brown spurned it. *Since his sentence*, and since the decision on the appeal, one of his counsel, Samuel Chilton, Esq., has filed with me a number of affidavits professing to *show grounds for delaying execution, in order to give time to make an issue of fact as to the sanity of the prisoner.* How such an issue can now, after sentence, confirmed by the court of appeals, be made, I am ignorant; but it is sufficient to say that I had repeatedly seen and conversed with the prisoner, and had just returned from a visit to him, when this appeal to me was put into my hands. As well as I can know the state of mind of anyone, I know that he was sane, and remarkably sane, if quick and clear perception; if assumed rational premises, and consecutive reasoning from them; if cautious tact in avoiding disclosures, and in covering conclusions and inferences; if memory and conception and practical common sense, and if composure and self-possession are evidences of a sound state of mind. He was more sane than his prompters and promoters, and concealed well the secret which made him seem to do an act of mad impulse, by leaving him without his backers at Harpers Ferry; but he did not conceal his contempt for the cowardice which did not back him better than with a plea of insanity, which he spurned to put in on his trial at Charlestown.

As to the second ground of appeal: I know of no magnanimity which is inhumane, and no inhumanity could well exceed that to our society, *our slaves* as well as their masters, which would turn felons like these, proud and defiant in their guilt, loose again on a border already torn by a fanatical and sectional strife which threatens the liberties of the white even more than it does the bondage of the black race.

As to the third ground: Is it true that the due execution of our laws, fairly and justly administered upon these confessed robbers, murderers and traitors, will make them martyrs in the public sentiments of other states? If so, then it is time indeed that execution shall be done upon them, and that we should prepare in earnest for the "irrepressible conflict," with that sympathy which, in demanding for these criminals pardons and reprieves, and in wreaking vengeance for their refusal, would make criminals of us. Indeed, a blasphemous moral treason, an expressed fellow-feeling with felons, a professed conservatism of crime, a defiant and boastful guilty demoniac spirit combined, arraign us, the outraged community, as the wrong-doers who must do penance and prevent our penalty by pardon and reprieve of these martyrs. This sympathy sent these men, its mere tools, to do the deeds which sentenced them. It may have sent them to be martyrs for mischief's sake; but the execution of our laws is necessary to warn future victims not again to be its tools. To heed this outside clamor at all, was to grant at once unconditional grace. To hang would be no more martyrdom than to incarcerate the fanatic. The sympathy would have asked on and on for liberation, and to nurse and sooth him whilst life lasted, in prison. His state of health would have been heralded weekly as from a palace; visitors would have come effectively reverent, to see the *shorn* felon at his "hard labor"; the work of his hands would have been sought as holy relics; and his party-colored dress would have become, perhaps, a uniform for the next band of impious marauders. There was no middle ground of mitigation. To pardon or reprieve at all, was to proclaim a licensed impunity to the thousand fanatics who are mad only in the guilt and folly of setting up their individual supremacy over law, life, property, and civil liberty itself. This sympathy with the leaders was worse than the invasion itself. The appeal was: it is policy to make *no martyrs*, but to disarm murderers, traitors, robbers, insurrectionists, by *free pardon* for wanton, malicious, unprovoked felons!

I could but ask, will execution of the legal sentence of a humane law make martyrs of such criminals? Do sectional and social masses hallow these crimes? Do whole communities sympathize with the outlaws, instead of sympathizing with the outraged society of a sister sovereignty? If so, then the sympathy is as felonious as the criminals, and is far more dangerous than was the invasion. The threat of martyrdom is a threat against our peace, and demands execution to defy such sympathy and such saints of martyrdom. The issue was forced upon us: Shall John Brown be pardoned, lest he might be canonized by execution of felony for confessed murder, robbery and treason in inciting servile insurrection in Virginia? Why a martyr? Because thousands applaud his acts and opinions, and glorify his crimes? Was I to hesitate after this? Sympathy was in insurrection, and had to be subdued more sternly than was John Brown. John Brown had surely to die according to law, and Virginia has to meet the issue. It is made. We have friends or we have not in the states whence these invaders come. They must now be not only *conservative* but *active* to prevent invaders coming. We are in arms.

Information from all quarters, with responsible names, and anonymous, dated the same time, from places far distant from each other, came, of organized conspiracies and combinations to obstruct our laws, to rescue and seize hostages, to commit rapine and burning along our borders on Maryland, Pennsylvania, Ohio and Indiana, proceeding from these states and from New York, Massachusetts and other states and Canada. These multiplied in every form for weeks; and at last, on the 19th of November, a call was very properly and timely made by Col. Davis for an additional force of 500 men.

These reports and rumors, from so many sources, of every character and form, so simultaneous, from places so far apart, at the game time, from persons so unlike in evidences of education, could be from no conspiracy to hoax; *but I relied not so much upon them as upon the earnest continued general appeal of sympathizers with the crimes. It was impossible for so much of such sympathy to exist without exciting bad men to action of rescue or revenge.* On this I *acted. . . .*

We must, then, acknowledge and act on the fact that present relations between the states cannot be permitted longer to exist without abolishing slavery throughout the United States, or compelling us to defend it by force of arms. . . .

15

U.S. SENATE SELECT COMMITTEE ON THE HARPERS FERRY INVASION

The Mason Report

June 15, 1860

Less than two weeks after John Brown's execution for treason against the state of Virginia, the U.S. Senate appointed a bipartisan five-man committee to investigate the Harpers Ferry raid and to determine precisely who contributed the money, weapons, and ammunition. Virginia's states' rights Senator James Mason — a lead author of the 1850 Fugitive Slave

U.S. Senate Committee Reports, 1859–1860, II, 1–19.

Law and powerful chairman of the Senate Foreign Relations Committee—
chaired the committee and submitted this majority report. Other mem-
bers of the majority of the five-man committee who signed the report were
Senator Jefferson Davis of Mississippi, the future president of the Confed-
erate States of America, and Senator Graham Fitch of Indiana, a Demo-
cratic ally of President James Buchanan.

The committee heard testimony from thirty-two witnesses, and the
majority Democrats tried in vain to use the evidence to implicate promi-
nent Republicans in the raid and prove their involvement in a vast con-
spiracy. Failing to prove this, they used their majority report to imply
strongly that John Brown's actions were the result of dangerous Republi-
can party doctrines. For their part, Republicans did their best to distance
themselves from Brown and his actions, and their two members of the
committee refused to sign the majority report.

In the Senate of the United States, Mr. Mason submitted the following
report.

The Select Committee of the Senate appointed to inquire into the late
invasion and seizure of the public property at Harpers Ferry beg leave to
submit their report.

On the 14th of December, 1859, the resolutions annexed were
adopted by the Senate of the United States:

Resolved, That a committee be appointed to inquire into the facts
attending the late invasion and seizure of the armory and arsenal of
the United States at Harpers Ferry, in Virginia, by a band of armed
men, and report—

Whether the same was attended by armed resistance to the
authorities and public force of the United States, and by the murder
of any of the citizens of Virginia, or of any troops sent there to protect the public property;

Whether such invasion and seizure was made under color of any
organization intended to subvert the government of any of the
States of the Union; what was the character and extent of such organization; and whether any citizens of the United States not present
were implicated therein, or accessory thereto, by contributions of
money, arms, munitions, or otherwise;

What was the character and extent of the military equipment in
the hands or under the control of said armed band; and where and
how and when the same was obtained and transported to the place
so invaded.

That said committee report whether any and what legislation may, in their opinion, be necessary on the part of the United States for the future preservation of the peace of the country, or for the safety of the public property; and that said committee have power to send for persons and papers. . . .

There will be found in the Appendix, a copy of the proceedings of a convention held at Chatham, in Canada, before referred to, of the provisional form of government there pretended to have been instituted, the object of which clearly was to subvert the government of one or more of the States, and of course to that extent the government of the United States. The character of the military organization is shown by the commissions issued to certain of the armed party as captains, lieutenants, etc., a specimen of which will be found in the Appendix. It clearly appeared that the scheme of Brown was to take with him comparatively few men, but those had been carefully trained by military instruction previously, and were to act as officers. For his military force he relied, very clearly, on inciting insurrection amongst the slaves, who he supposed would flock to him as soon as it became known that he had entered the State and had been able to retain his position—an expectation to no extent realized, though it was owing alone to the loyalty and well-affected disposition of the slaves that he did not succeed in inciting a servile war, with its necessary attendants of rapine and murder of all sexes, ages, and conditions. It is very certain from the proofs before the committee, that not one of the captured slaves, although arms were placed in their hands, attempted to use them; but on the contrary, as soon as their safety would admit, in the absence of their captors, their arms were thrown away and they hastened back to their homes.

It is shown that Brown brought with him for this expedition arms sufficient to have placed an effective weapon in the hands of not less than 1,500 men; besides which, had he succeded in obtaining the aid he looked to from the slaves, he had entirely under his control all the arms of the United States deposited in the arsenal at Harpers Ferry. After his capture, beside the arms he brought in the wagon to the Ferry, there were found on the Maryland side, where he had left them, 200 Sharp's rifled carbines, and 200 revolver pistols, packed in the boxes of the manufacturers, with 900 or 1,000 pikes, carefully and strongly made, the blade of steel being securely riveted to a handle about five feet in length; many thousand percussion caps in boxes, and ample stores of fixed ammunition, besides a large supply of powder in kegs, and a chest that contained hospital and other military stores, beside a quantity of extra clothing for troops.

For an answer to the inquiry, how far "any citizens of the United States, not present, were implicated therein or accessory thereto by contributions of money, arms, munitions, or otherwise," the committee deem it best to refer to the evidence which accompanies this report. It does not appear that such contributions were made with actual knowledge of the use for which they were designed by Brown, although it does appear that money was freely contributed by those styling themselves friends of this man Brown, and friends alike of what they styled "the cause of freedom" (of which they claimed him to be an especial apostle) without inquiry as to the way in which the money would be used by him to advance such pretended cause. The evidence fully shows that he had the pikes manufactured in Connecticut especially for this expedition, and certainly they would appear to have been the most formidable weapon which could have been placed in the unskillful hands for which they were intended. For a description of this weapon, and the story told to the manufacturer by Brown when he ordered them, the committee refer to the evidence of the latter. They were sent directly from Connecticut to Brown under his assumed name of Isaac Smith, first to Chambersburg, in Pennsylvania, there received by some of Brown's men, who were placed there also under assumed names, and by whom they were transported to his abode near Harpers Ferry.

The history of the rifles and pistols is most interesting to this inquiry. It appears from the evidence that, in 1856, these 200 Sharp's carbines had been forwarded by an association in Massachusetts called the "*Massachusetts State Kansas Committee*," at first to Chicago, on their way to Kansas. At Chicago they were placed under the control of another association, called the "*National Kansas Aid Committee.*" There being some difficulty, from the disordered condition of the country at that time, in getting them to Kansas, they were sent by this last named association into Iowa, where they remained. In January, 1857, it seems there was a meeting of this National Kansas Committee in the city of New York. That committee was constituted of one member from most of the non-slaveholding States. At that meeting John Brown appeared, and made application to have these arms placed in his possession. It would seem that he wanted them, as he expressed it, "for purposes of defense in Kansas"; but as the troubles there were nearly ended, such pretension seems to have been discredited by those to whom it was addressed.

At page 245 of the testimony, a full account of this application for the arms will be found, as given by H. B. Hurd, who was the secretary of the association. He states that, "When Mr. Brown was pressing his claim for the aid desired, I asked him this question: 'If you get the arms and money you desire, will you invade Missouri or any slave Territory?' to which he replied, 'I am no adventurer; you all know me; you are acquainted with my history; you know what I have done in Kansas; I do not expose my plans; no one knows them but myself, except, perhaps, one; I do not wish to be interrogated; if you wish to give me anything, I want you to give it freely; I have no other purpose but to serve the cause of liberty.' " And he also adds: "Although it had been understood by the members of the committee that Mr. Brown intended to arm one hundred men, to be scattered about in the Territory and to be actual settlers, and engaged in their several pursuits, only to be called out to repel invasion or defend the Kansas free-State settlers, yet this reply was not satisfactory to all, and the arms were voted back to your committee" (meaning the Massachusetts State Kansas Committee) "to be disposed of as you thought best."

How and why these arms (the 200 Sharp's rifles) were originally purchased by this Massachusetts State Kansas Committee, will appear from the testimony of George L. Stearns, who was its president or chairman, at page 227 of the testimony. It is shown by Hurd that, after the national committee, for the reason stated, had refused to intrust them to Brown, on his application, they "were voted back," as Hurd calls it, to the Massachusetts State Kansas Committee; and, on page 229 of the testimony, will be found a letter from Stearns to Brown, dated at Boston, on the 8th of January, 1857, advising him that he was directed by his committee to send him an order on Edward Clark, of Lawrence, in Kansas Territory, for the two hundred rifles, "with four thousand ball cartridges, thirty-one military caps" (afterwards corrected as thirty-one thousand percussion caps) which he states were then stored at Tabor, in Iowa, with directions to hold the same as agent of the society, subject to their order, and, at the same time, authorizing him to draw on their treasurer, at Boston, for a sum of money not to exceed five hundred dollars. At page 228 of the testimony will be found the following question, put to Stearns, with his answer:

Question: "Was it at Brown's request that you put him in possession of these arms in January, 1857?"

Answer: "No, sir; but because we needed an agent to secure them," &c.

And again, at page 230, he was asked: "Did I understand you to say that this was voluntarily proffered to him, and not at his request?" (Meaning the arms.)

Answer: "Yes, sir."

Question: "Why did you desire to place these arms in his possession?"

Answer: "For safe-keeping."

Question: "Were they not in safe-keeping where they were?"

Answer: "They were not substantially in our hands. We had passed them into the hands of the National Kansas Committee, to be transported to Kansas," &c.

The committee are not disposed to draw harsh, or perhaps uncharitable conclusions; yet they cannot fail to remark that these arms, which had been refused to Brown by the national committee, for the very satisfactory reason that he gave evasive answers to their inquiry how they were to be used, were proffered to him, and without request on his part, by the Massachusetts committee; and this proffer is found attended by the fact, not a little to be remarked, that contemporaneous with it—that is to say, in January, 1857—this Mr. Stearns gave authority to Brown to purchase from the Massachusetts Arms Company two hundred revolver pistols, which Stearns alleges he paid for out of his own funds . . . giving to Brown at the same time authority to draw on him at sight for $7,000, "in sums as it might be wanted, for the subsistence of one hundred men, provided that it should be necessary at any time to call that number into the field for active service in the defense of Kansas, in 1857." Considering the comparative tranquil condition of Kansas at the period referred to, it is not easy to reconcile this act of the "Massachusetts State Kansas Committee" and its chairman with a reasonable regard to the peace of the country, or the lives of their fellow-citizens. These arms, however, with the two hundred rifles, were left from that time in Brown's possession, although as stated by the witness Stearns, at page 228 of the testimony, "the exigency contemplated did not occur," and therefore no part of the $7,000 was drawn by Brown.

At what time Brown procured the pistols, or transported them to the West, appears only from the testimony of Stearns, who says he paid for them, and the freight on them to Iowa, on production to him of the railroad receipt afterwards, in 1858, but it does not appear that they were sent along with the Sharp's rifles from Ohio to him, in the neighborhood of Harpers Ferry. In 1858, Brown, it appears, told Stearns that both the rifles and the pistols were then "stored in Ohio."

(Page 232 of the testimony.) From the correspondence of John Brown, Jr., signing himself "John Smith," with his father, and with J. H. Kagi (under the name of "J. Henrie") shortly before the invasion at Harpers Ferry, printed in the Appendix, it will be seen that they were sent by him from Ashtabula County, Ohio, to his father at Harpers Ferry, *via* Chambersburg.

The testimony of the witnesses, Hurd and Stearns, would show that the arms refused to Brown by the national committee, had been *afterwards* voted to him by the Massachusetts committee—reference to Hurd's statement (page 250) and to the order given by Stearns to Brown (page 234) for the arms, would from their dates seem to contradict this, but only as to the order of time. The facts interesting to this inquiry are only, were the arms placed under control of Brown; by whom; and when? and this is clearly shown.

It is shown fully, from the testimony, that, although Brown when he first went to Kansas was accompanied by two of his sons, with their families, yet that he never removed his family from New York, and that he subsequently freely and fully avowed that he never had an idea of settling in Kansas, but was attracted to remain there only in the hope that by keeping alive the irritation and excited feeling of the settlers on the subject of slavery, and stimulating and accustoming them to war and bloodshed, he would be enabled in some way to lead them across the borders to incite a servile war in Missouri, from whence he might be able to extend it to other slaveholding States. Ultimately disappointed in this, and so early as the fall of 1857, he seems to have conceived the plan of a distinct invasion of one of the slaveholding States, under the organization and in the manner in which it was afterwards carried into execution in Virginia. This, of course, required the command of large sums of money; and he seems to have so successfully impressed himself and his capacity for conducting what he and his associates styled "the cause of freedom," upon the sickly, if not depraved, sensibilities of his allies in such "cause," as to command their confidence, if he did not altogether lull their suspicions. Letters to and from Brown and others, in the Appendix, give much insight into the manner and the sources whence his funds were derived.

The testimony shows generally how these contributions were made—occasionally in large sums paid directly to Brown, but more usually by collections made in the villages and towns throughout the country by itinerant lecturers. These lectures appear to have been patronized by the principal men in the States where they were delivered. Their topics were various, but all directed in some manner to what was called "the general cause of freedom"; sometimes for the creation of a fund to aid fugitive slaves in their escape; at other times with no definite character ascribed to them, except that the funds collected were to be used in promoting human freedom; and at other times, as would seem, for the personal expenses or to reimburse supposed losses of Brown. See the evidence of J. R. Giddings, pages 150, 151, and 152, of the testimony. He was a lecturer through the Northwestern States, one class of his lectures devoted, as he states, to "an exposition of the doctrines of the higher law," and which he expounds, at page 151 of the testimony, thus:

> What I mean by the higher law is, that power which for the last two centuries has been proclaimed by the philosophers and jurists and statesmen of Germany, Europe, and the United States, called, in other words, the law of nature; by which we suppose that God, in giving man his existence, gave him the right to exist; the right to breathe vital air; the right to enjoy the light of the sun; to drink the waters of the earth; to unfold his moral nature; to learn the laws that control his moral and physical being; to bring himself into harmony with those laws, and enjoy that happiness which is consequent on such obedience. . . .

As a further exposition of the views entertained by those devotees to the so-styled "cause for freedom," the committee refer to the evidence of George L. Stearns, at page 240. This gentleman, although not a lecturer, was, as shown by his testimony, one of the most active and successful workers in that "cause." For his views as to the legitimate use of money contributed to this "cause," see page 242, where he states:

> From first to last, I understood John Brown to be a man who was opposed to slavery, and, as such, that he would take every opportunity to free slaves where he could; I did not know in what way; I only knew that from the fact of his having done it in Missouri in the instance referred to; I furnished him with money because I considered him as one who would be of use in case such troubles arose as had arisen previously in Kansas; that was my object in furnishing the money; I did not ask him what he was to do with it, nor did I suppose he would do anything that I should disapprove.

To the question "Do you disapprove of such a transaction as that at Harpers Ferry," he answered: "I should have disapproved of it if I had known it; but I have since changed my opinion; I believe John Brown to be the representative man of this century, as Washington was of the last—the Harpers Ferry affair, and the capacity shown by the Italians for self-government, the great events of this age. One will free Europe, and the other America."

And so in the testimony of Samuel G. Howe, a physician of Boston. At page 166, speaking of Brown, he says: "I contributed to his aid at various times."

Question: "His aid in what way?"

Answer: "In the same way that I contributed to the aid of other anti-slavery men; men who give up their occupations, their industry, to write papers or to deliver lectures, or otherwise to propagate anti-slavery sentiments. I give as much money every year as I can possibly afford. I am in the habit of contributing in that way."

And at page 167:

Question: "Will you state what you mean by that phrase 'contributing for the promotion of anti-slavery sentiments?' What is the meaning of that idea?"

Answer: "In the same way that I would promote the Gospel among the heathens; I cannot precisely say what. The means are various—lectures, writing, talking, discussing the matter."

Question: "What ends are to be attained by promoting that anti-slavery sentiment? What is the object in view?"

Answer: "The promotion of freedom among men; the same object as the fathers in the revolution."

Question: "Was one of its objects the means of attaining the freedom of the African slaves held in this country?"

Answer: "That would be the natural and desired result."

Question: "Was that one of the ends to be attained by promoting this anti-slavery sentiment by lecturing and otherwise?"

Answer: "It was. I answer these questions out of courtesy to the Chairman, but I must think they are rather wide."

Of these three witnesses, one, Giddings, represented a district in the House of Representatives from Ohio for a long series of years, and is known to the country as an intelligent man; another, Dr. Howe, holds the highest professional and social position in the city of Boston. The other, Mr. Stearns, is a merchant in the same city, of wealth and with all the influence usually attending it. With such elements at work, unchecked by law and not rebuked but encouraged by public opinion, with money freely contributed and placed in irresponsible hands, it may easily be seen how this expedition to excite servile war in one of the States of the Union was got up, and it may equally be seen how like expeditions may certainly be anticipated in future whenever desperadoes offer themselves to carry them into execution. In regard to the one here inquired into, it appears that Brown, after the dispersal of his convention at Chatham, proceeded to the eastern States to provide materials both of arms and money; and in reference to the ease with which the latter was obtained without scrutiny as to the uses to which it was to be put, it will stand upon the record as a remarkable fact, that a check for one hundred dollars given by Gerrit Smith to Brown was handed by him directly, in part payment to the manufacturer of the pikes with which the slaves were to have been armed. This gentleman, Mr. Smith, is known to the country as a man of large wealth and a liberal contributor to this pretended "cause." By reason of his very infirm health he was not summoned as a witness before the committee; and the use of this particular check is not referred to as proof in any manner that its contributor knew definitely what was to be done with it, but it is referred to as a most persuasive proof of the utter insecurity of the peace and safety of some of the States of this Union, in the existing condition of the public mind and its purposes in the nonslaveholding States. It may not become the committee to suggest a duty in those States to provide by proper legislation against machinations by their citizens or within their borders destructive of the peace of their confederate republics; but it does become them fully to expose the consequences resulting from the present license there existing, because the peace and integrity of the Union is necessarily involved in its continuance. . . .

The history of the large armament collected by Brown at Harpers Ferry is thus clearly traced. The rifled carbines, manufactured in Connecticut, intended, as would appear, to be originally used in intestine strife in Kansas, and sent there for that purpose, were voluntarily, by the Massachusetts Kansas Committee, through its chairman, placed in the hands of Brown, with vague and inexplicit instructions as to their use, about the time when it would appear that he finally conceived the purpose of exciting servile war in some of the slaveholding States. They were allowed to remain in his possession, notwithstanding his failure or refusal to give them up after that committee and its chairman had been warned of his purpose to put them to some use not warranted by those who owned them. The revolver pistols, as shown by the testimony of Stearns, chairman of that committee, was a volunteer gift from him to Brown, at about the same time the carbines were handed over to him, and whether thus beyond his control or not, were not recalled from his possession. The expedition, so atrocious in its character, would have been arrested, had even ordinary care been taken on the part of the Massachusetts committee to ascertain whether Brown was truthful in his professions. Even the modest inquiry made of him by the National Kansas Committee, as stated by their secretary, Hurd, resulted in such equivocation and evasion on his part as led them peremptorily to refuse these arms to him, as their act.

The facts exposed in this part of the testimony speak for themselves. It will be remembered that the period referred to, when Mr. Wilson communicated his suspicions to Dr. Howe, and through him to the chairman of the Massachusetts committee, was so late as May, 1858. Order had then been restored in Kansas. The troops of the United States had been long previously withdrawn, and the only contests remaining in the Territory were conducted through the ballot-box. Notwithstanding all which, it would seem Brown was to be kept afoot, intrusted with arms for military organization, and amply supplied with money. The testimony shows that after his treasonable proceedings at Chatham he went back to New England, traveled through its several villages, collecting money, which was freely contributed under the auspices both of Dr. Howe and Mr. Chairman Stearns and others, with a knowledge that he retained the large supply of arms of which they had failed to dispossess him.

Upon the whole testimony, there can be no doubt that Brown's plan was to commence a servile war on the borders of Virginia, which he expected to extend, and which he believed his means and resources were sufficient to extend through that State and throughout the entire South. Upon being questioned, soon after his capture, by the Governor of Virginia, as to his plans, he rather indignantly repelled the idea that it was to be limited to collecting and protecting the slaves until they could be sent out of the State as fugitives. On the contrary, he vehemently insisted that his purpose was to retain them on the soil, to put arms in their hands, with which he came provided for the purpose, and to use them as his soldiery. (Pages 6, 62.)

This man (Brown) was uniformly spoken of, by those who seemed best to have known him, as of remarkable reticence in his habits, or, as they expressed it, "secretive." It does not appear that he intrusted even his immediate followers with his plans, fully, even after they were ripe for execution. Nor have the committee been enabled clearly to trace knowledge of them to any. The only exception would seem to be in the instance of the anonymous letter received by the Secretary of War in the summer preceding the attack, referred to in the testimony.

The Secretary shows that he could get no clue to the writer; nor were the committee enabled in any way to trace him. Considering that the letter was anonymous, as well as vague and apparently incoherent in its statements, it was not at all remarkable, in the opinion of the committee, that it did not arrest the attention of the officer to whom it was addressed.

The point chosen for the attack seems to have been selected from the two-fold inducement of the security afforded the invaders by a mountain country, and the large deposit of arms in the arsenal of the United States there situated. It resulted in the murder of three most respectable citizens of the State of Virginia without cause, and in the like murder of an unoffending free negro. Of the military force brought against them, one marine was killed and one wounded; whilst eight of the militia and other forces of the neighborhood were wounded, with more or less severity, in the several assaults made by them.

Of the list of "insurgents" given in Colonel Lee's report (fourteen whites and five negroes) Brown, Stevens, and Coppic, of the whites, with Shields Green, and Copeland, of the negroes, captured at the storming of the engine-house, were subsequently executed in Virginia, after judicial trial; as were also John E. Cook and Albert Hazlett, who at first escaped, but were captured in Pennsylvania and delivered up for trial to the authorities of Virginia—making in all seven thus executed. It does not seem to have been very clearly ascertained how many of the party escaped. Brown stated that his party consisted of twenty-two in number. Seven were executed, ten were killed at the Ferry; thus leaving five to be accounted for. Four of these five, it is believed, were left on the Maryland side in charge of the arms when Brown crossed the river, and who could not afterwards join him; leaving but one, who, as it would appear, is the only survivor of the party who accompanied Brown across the river, and whose escape is not accounted for.

The committee, after much consideration, are not prepared to suggest any legislation, which, in their opinion, would be adequate to prevent like occurrences in the future. The only provisions in the Constitution of the United States which would seem to import any authority in the government of the United States to interfere on occasions affecting the peace or safety of the States, are found in the eighth section of the first article, amongst the powers of Congress, "to provide for calling for the militia to execute the laws of the Union, suppress insurrections, and repel invasions"; and in the fourth section of the fourth article, in the following words: "The United States shall guaranty to every State in this Union a republican form of government, and shall protect each of them against invasion, and, on the application of the legislature or of the executive (when the legislature cannot be convened) against domestic violence." The "invasion" here spoken of would seem to import an invasion by the public force of a foreign power, or (if not so limited and equally referable to an invasion by one State of another) still it would seem that public force, or force exercised under the sanction of acknowledged political power, is there meant. The invasion (to call it so) by Brown and his followers at Harpers Ferry, was in no sense of that character. It was simply the act of lawless ruffians, under the sanction of no public or political authority—distinguishable only from ordinary felonies by the ulterior ends in contemplation by them, and by the fact that the money to maintain the expedition, and the large armament they brought with them, had been contributed and furnished by the citizens of other States of the Union, under circumstances that must continue to jeopard the safety and peace of the Southern States, and against which Congress has no power to legislate.

If the several States, whether from motives of policy or a desire to preserve the peace of the Union, if not from fraternal feeling, do not hold it incumbent on them, after the experience of the country, to guard in future by appropriate legislation against occurrences similar to the one here inquired into, the committee can find no guarantee elsewhere for the security of peace between the States of the Union.

So far, however, as the safety of the public property is involved, the committee would earnestly recommend that provision should be made by the executive, or, if necessary, by law, to keep under adequate military guard the public armories and arsenals of the United States, in some way after the manner practised at the navy-yards and forts.

Before closing their report, the committee deem it proper to state that four persons summoned as witnesses, to wit: John Brown, Jr., of Ohio, James Redpath, of Massachusetts, Frank B. Sanborn, of Massachusetts, and Thaddeus Hyatt, of New York, failing or refusing to appear before the committee, warrants were issued by order of the Senate for their arrest. Of these, Thaddeus Hyatt only was arrested; and on his appearance before the Senate, still refusing obedience to the summons of the committee, he was by order of the Senate committed to the jail of the District of Columbia. In regard to the others, it appeared by the return of the marshal of the northern district of Ohio, as deputy of the Sergeant-at-Arms, that John Brown, Jr., at first evaded the process of the Senate, and afterwards, with a number of other persons, armed themselves to prevent his arrest. The marshal further reported in his return that Brown could not be arrested unless he was authorized in like manner to employ force. Sanborn was arrested by a deputy of the Sergeant-at-Arms, and afterwards released from custody by the judges of the supreme court of Massachusetts on *habeas corpus*. Redpath, by leaving his State, or otherwise concealing himself, successfully evaded the process of the Senate.

And the committee ask to be discharged from the further consideration of the subject.

J. M. Mason
Chairman
Jeff'n Davis
G. N. Fitch

16

WILLIAM W. PATTON

John Brown's Body

1862

Early in the Civil War, a group of Boston volunteer militiamen—which included a Scottish tenor named John Brown—set humorous words to a tune probably written by William Steffe in the mid-1850s. Intended as a joke on the very much alive Scottish John Brown, the song was sung on numerous occasions in 1861. Audiences assumed, of course, that the song was inspired by the recently executed John Brown of Osawatomie, whose actions at Harpers Ferry had done so much to bring on the war between the states. During the conflict, countless new verses were added that pertained to the more famous John Brown, including the version printed here (written by the Reverend William W. Patton in 1862).

During a visit to Washington in 1861, the poet Julia Ward Howe— an acquaintance of John Brown's—was inspired by the song to write

"John Brown Song," J. Wrigley. Publisher, of Songs, Ballads, and Toy Books &c., No. 27 Chatham Street (Opposite City Hall Park) New York. [n.d.] New York, New York. J. Wrigley "No. 964."

new lyrics to the popular tune. Her "Battle Hymn of the Republic" was published in the Atlantic Monthly *in 1862. The song is but one of the ways John Brown's story—with the Harpers Ferry raid as its defining element—has been passed down to generations of Americans.*

John Brown's body lies a mouldering in the grave,
While weep the sons of bondage, whom he ventured all to save,
But tho' he lost his life in struggling for the slave,
 His soul is marching on.

  Chorus—Glory, Glory Hallelujah!
     Glory, Glory Hallelujah!
     Glory, Glory Hallelujah!
     His soul is marching on.

John Brown was a hero undaunted, true, and brave,
And Kansas knew his valor, when he fought her rights to save:
And now though the grass grows green above his grave,
 His soul is marching on. Glory, &c.

He captured Harpers Ferry with his nineteen men so few,
And he frighten'd old Virginny till she trembled through and through:
They hung him for a traitor; themselves a traitor crew,
 But his soul is marching on. Glory, &c.

John Brown was John the Baptist, of Christ we are to see,
Christ who of the bondman shall the Liberator be,
And soon throughout the sunny South, the slaves shall all be free,
 For his soul is marching on. Glory, &c.

The conflict that he heralded, he looks from heaven to view,
On the army of the Union, with his flag Red, White and Blue;
And heaven shall ring with anthems, o'er the deed they mean to do
 For his soul is marching on. Glory, &c.

Ye soldiers of Freedom, then strike, while strike ye may,
The death-blow of oppression in a better time and way;
For the dawn of old John Brown, has brightened into day.
 And his soul is marching on. Glory, &c.

A Chronology of John Brown and Events of the Civil War (1800–1865)

1800   John Brown is born in Torrington, Connecticut, on May 9, to Owen and Ruth Mills Brown.

1805   The Brown family moves to Hudson, Ohio.

1812   Twelve-year-old John Brown travels alone one hundred miles through Ohio and Michigan during wartime to deliver a herd of cattle. En route he witnesses an enslaved black boy being beaten with a shovel and recalls the memory as making him into a "determined Abolitionist."

1816   John Brown makes a formal profession of faith and joins his father's Congregational church in Hudson. He also leaves home to study at a Massachusetts preparatory school. His formal education ends the following year.

1820   John Brown marries Dianthe Lusk on June 21. He decides to support his family by learning the surveyor's trade.

1826   The Browns move to New Richmond, Pennsylvania. John Brown opens a tannery.

1831   William Lloyd Garrison establishes *The Liberator* and calls for an immediate end to slavery on January 1. On August 22 Nat Turner leads the nation's largest slave uprising in Southampton County, Virginia, killing seventy whites. More than one hundred African Americans are executed or killed in the uprising's aftermath.

1832   Dianthe Brown dies three days after giving birth to a stillborn child.

1833   John Brown marries sixteen-year-old Mary Day. In addition to the five children John Brown brought to his second marriage, the couple had thirteen more children. Oberlin College is founded in Ohio and admits both white and black students.

1837   In the aftermath of the murder of abolitionist editor Elijah Love-joy, John Brown (having recently relocated to Franklin Mills, Ohio) stands in a church and dedicates himself to the destruction of slavery. A financial panic ensnares the Brown family in financial difficulty.

1840   John Brown declares bankruptcy and returns to Hudson, Ohio. Two years later a court strips him of most of his possessions.

1844   The Brown family moves to Akron, Ohio, and Brown enters into a business partnership with Simon Perkins to sell wool.

1846   John Brown moves to Springfield, Massachusetts, to run his wool business. New York philanthropist Gerrit Smith deeds some of his less-desirable land in remote Franklin and Essex counties to the state's free blacks.

1847   John Brown meets the black abolitionist Frederick Douglass.

1848   John Brown composes "Sambo's Mistakes" in the black-owned newspaper *Ram's Horn*; acquires 244 acres from Smith in remote North Elba, New York; and agrees to help "instruct" the community's black residents.

1849   John Brown travels throughout western Europe in an attempt to sell wool at high prices; the trip is a financial disaster.

1850   The federal Fugitive Slave Law enrages abolitionists and many moderate Northerners. John Brown preaches against the law in November.

1851   John Brown organizes the otherwise all-black United States League of Gileadites in Springfield to defend against slave catchers empowered by the Fugitive Slave Law to return — or "render"—runaways to slavery.

1854   Congress passes the Kansas-Nebraska Act, which opens vast new territories to white settlement and casts aside the thirty-one-year-old Missouri Compromise, which prohibited slavery in the former Louisiana Purchase north of 36°30′. John Brown's unmarried sons Frederick, Salmon, and Owen go to Kansas to acquire land and try to prevent slavery from establishing itself in the territory. They found "Brown's Station" near the settlement of Osawatomie.

1855   Jason and John Brown Jr. join their brothers in Kansas; John Brown decides to come to Kansas in June. In December the Browns and their antislavery allies defend Lawrence from an invading army from Missouri in the Wakarusa War.

1856   *May 21*:   The free-state town of Lawrence, Kansas, is sacked by a proslavery army.

May 22: Antislavery Senator Charles Sumner is caned nearly to death on the floor of the Capitol by a proslavery congressman.

May 24: John Brown leads a nocturnal expedition that results in the murders of five proslavery settlers living near Pottawatomie Creek.

June 2: Brown defeats and captures a larger proslavery force at the Battle of Black Jack.

August 30: Brown's men fail to defend the free-state town of Osawatomie against a much larger force; Frederick Brown dies in the battle.

1857   Brown travels throughout New England to raise funds and arms for the struggle in Kansas, and meets the wealthy and well-connected men known as the "Secret Six," who finance his antislavery efforts. The Supreme Court rules in *Dred Scott v. Sandford* that blacks—free or enslaved—are not citizens of the United States and the Missouri Compromise (or any other congressional act restricting slavery in the territories) is unconstitutional.

1858   Brown calls for a convention of the "Oppressed People of the United States" to meet in Chatham, Ontario, on May 8. At the meeting Brown unveils his plan to attack slavery in Virginia and presents his Provisional Constitution for a new free state in the South for ratification. On December 20, Brown rides into Missouri and attacks two proslavery homesteads, confiscating property and liberating eleven slaves.

1859   *January–March*: John Brown leads the liberated slaves on an eighty-two-day trek to freedom in Canada.

July 3: Using the name Isaac Smith, Brown rents the Kennedy farm in western Maryland, five miles from the federal arsenal at Harpers Ferry, Virginia. The rest of the raiding party arrives over the ensuing months for training.

August 16: At a clandestine meeting at a quarry near Chambersburg, Pennsylvania, Frederick Douglass declines Brown's exhortation to join the raiding party.

October 16: Brown leads the raiding party into Harpers Ferry, where they quickly capture the armory, the arsenal, and rifle works. They also take many local citizens and militia members hostage.

October 17: After Brown lets an eastbound train proceed toward Baltimore, the conductor alerts the authorities that Harpers Ferry is under attack. President James Buchanan orders Lieutenant Colonel Robert E. Lee and a band of U.S. Marines to retake the town. Local militiamen pour into the town and engage in numerous attacks on Brown and his men.

October 18: Lee and the Marines under his command breach the enginehouse where Brown and his men have holed up; Brown surrenders.

October 25–November 2: Brown stands trial in Charles Town and is found guilty of murder, inciting insurrection, and treason against the state of Virginia. He is sentenced to death.

November 2–December 2: John Brown writes and answers many letters from his prison cell. After their publication more Northerners are sympathetic toward Brown and his actions.

December 2: John Brown dies on the gallows in Charles Town.

1861 Confederate guns fire on Fort Sumter on April 12, igniting the Civil War.

1865 The ratification of the Thirteenth Amendment to the Constitution abolishes slavery in the United States.

Questions for Consideration

1. Describe John Brown's family and childhood. What are the central facts of his early life?

2. What are the religious beliefs and practices of the Brown family? Are they similar or different from mainstream American religious beliefs at the time?

3. What events early in John Brown's life influenced his ideas about slavery?

4. How did John Brown's experiences as a businessman affect his family life? His career as an abolitionist?

5. What was John Brown's relationship with the abolitionist movement?

6. Describe John Brown's ideas about race. How did they differ—and how did they reflect—mainstream American racial ideas in the nineteenth century?

7. John Brown believed the federal government was run by, and for, slaveholders. Why did he think this? Was he correct?

8. Why did Kansas "bleed" in the mid-1850s?

9. Is it surprising that John Brown found such powerful and important allies for his antislavery schemes?

10. Was John Brown's plan to foment slave rebellion in the Appalachian Mountains a workable one?

11. Why didn't throngs of slaves join Brown and his raiders to fight for their freedom?

12. Did John Brown get a fair trial after his capture at Harpers Ferry?

13. What did the raid accomplish? Do you regard it as successful or unsuccessful? By what criteria is it appropriate to judge success or failure?

14. Would John Brown have been as famous—or as historically significant—if he had died from his wounds on the floor of the enginehouse at Harpers Ferry?

15. How was John Brown so successful at "reinventing" himself from his prison cell in Charles Town?

16. Is John Brown a hero and a martyr? Or a murderer and a terrorist?

17. Why over the past 150 years have African Americans held John Brown in higher esteem than white Americans?

18. In what ways was antebellum America changed by John Brown's assault at Harpers Ferry?

19. Is violence, even for a good cause, ever justified? What about terror?

20. Did John Brown cause the Civil War, or even hasten its beginning?

21. Why should twenty-first-century Americans be interested in studying John Brown's raid?

Selected Bibliography

MANUSCRIPT COLLECTIONS

John Brown Papers, 1826–1948, Kansas State Historical Society.
Boyd B. Stutler Collection, microfilm, Ohio Historical Society.
Correspondence of John Brown Jr., Ohio Historical Society.
Kansas Collection, Spencer Research Library, University of Kansas.
State Department Territorial Papers: Kansas, 1854–1861 (microcopy No. 218, National Archives and Records Service).

COLLECTIONS OF BROWN'S WRITINGS

Ruchames, Louis, ed. *A John Brown Reader*. New York: Abelard-Schuman, 1959.
Sanborn, Franklin B. *Life and Letters of John Brown, Liberator of Kansas, and Martyr of Virginia*. Boston: Roberts Brothers, 1885.
Trodd, Zoe, and John Stauffer, eds. *Meteor of War: The John Brown Story*. Maplecrest, N.Y.: Brandywine Press, 2004.

OTHER PRIMARY SOURCES

Anderson, Osborne P. *A Voice from Harper's Ferry*. Boston: Printed for the Author, 1861.
Congressional Globe: Containing the Debates and Proceedings of the First Session of the Thirty-Sixth Congress, Also of the Special Session of the Senate. Vol. 1. Washington, D.C.: John C. Rives, 1860.
Dana, Richard H., Jr. "How We Met John Brown." *Atlantic Monthly*, 28 (July–Dec. 1871): 1–9.
Douglass, Frederick. *Life and Times of Frederick Douglass*. Boston: De Wolfe & Fiske Co., 1881, rev. 1892.
Emerson, Ralph Waldo. *Works: Journals and Miscellaneous Notebooks*, ed. Ronald A. Bosco and Glen Jackson. Cambridge, Mass.: Harvard University Press, 1982.
Quarles, Benjamin. *Blacks on John Brown*. Urbana: University of Illinois Press, 1972.

Sanborn, Franklin B. *Memoirs of John Brown*. Albany, N.Y.: J. Munsell, 1878.

Scheidenhelm, Richard, ed. *The Response to John Brown*. Belmont, Calif.: Wadsworth Publishing Company, 1972.

Thoreau, Henry David. *The Writings of Henry David Thoreau*. 20 vols. Boston: Houghton Mifflin, 1906.

Weiss, John. *The Life and Correspondence of Theodore Parker*. 2 vols. New York: D. Appleton, 1864.

Wise, Henry A. "Message to the Senate and House of Delegates of the General Assembly of the Commonwealth of Virginia." *Journal of the Senate and House of Delegates of the Commonwealth of Virginia: Begun and Held at the Capitol Session, 1859*. Richmond, Va.: James E. Goode, 1859.

BIOGRAPHIES AND OTHER CRITICAL WORKS

Aptheker, Herbert. *John Brown: American Martyr*. New York: New Century, 1960.

Bordewich, Fergus M. *Bound for Canaan: The Epic Story of the Underground Railroad and the War for the Soul of America*. New York: Amistad, 2005.

Boyer, Richard O. *The Legend of John Brown: A Biography and a History*. New York: Alfred A. Knopf, 1973.

Du Bois, W. E. B. *John Brown*. Philadelphia: G.W. Jacobs & Company, 1909.

Finkelman, Paul, ed. *His Soul Goes Marching On: Responses to John Brown and the Harper's Ferry Raid*. Charlottesville: University of Virginia Press, 1995.

Hugo, Victor. *John Brown*. Ridgewood, N.J.: Alwil Shop, 1902.

Iger, Eve M. *John Brown: His Soul Goes Marching On*. New York: Young Scott Books, 1969.

Malin, James C. *John Brown and the Legend of Fifty-six*. Philadelphia: The American Philosophical Society, 1942.

———. "The John Brown Legend in Pictures: Kissing the Negro Baby." *Kansas Historical Quarterly*, 8 (1939): 339–41; 9 (1940): 339–42.

Oates, Stephen B. *To Purge This Land with Blood: A Biography of John Brown*. New York: Harper & Row, 1970.

———. *Our Fiery Trial: Abraham Lincoln, John Brown, and the Civil War Era*. Amherst: University of Massachusetts Press, 1979.

Quarles, Benjamin. *Allies for Freedom: Blacks and John Brown*. New York: Oxford University Press, 1974.

Redpath, James. *Echoes of Harper's Ferry*. Boston: Thayer and Eldridge, 1860.

———. *The Public Life of Capt. John Brown*. Boston: Thayer and Eldridge, 1860.

Renehan, Edward. *The Secret Six: The True Tale of the Men Who Conspired with John Brown*. Columbia: University of South Carolina Press, 1997.

Reynolds, David S. *John Brown, Abolitionist: The Man Who Killed Slavery, Sparked the Civil War, and Seeded Civil Rights*. New York: Alfred A. Knopf, 2005.

Rossbach, Jeffrey S. *Ambivalent Conspirators: John Brown, the Secret Six, and a Theory of Slave Violence*. Philadelphia: University of Pennsylvania Press, 1982.

Scott, John Anthony, and Robert Alan Scott. *John Brown of Harper's Ferry*. New York: Facts on File, 1988.

Villard, Oswald Garrison. *John Brown, 1800–1859; A Biography Fifty Years After*. Boston: Houghton Mifflin, 1910.

Warren, Robert Penn. *John Brown: The Making of a Martyr*. New York: Payson & Clarke, 1929.

Wilson, Hill Peebles. *John Brown, Soldier of Fortune: A Critique*. Boston: The Cornhill Company, 1918.

Woodward, C. Vann. "John Brown's Private War," in *The Burden of Southern History*. Baton Rouge: Louisiana State University Press, 1960.

Index

abolitionists
  activities of, 1, 6, 45
  black, 5, 43–47
  Brown and, 3, 4, 5–10, 20, 32–33, 65–66
  Compromise of 1850 and, 11–12
  fear of, vii
  Fugitive Slave Law and, 11–12, 43
  funding of, 20, 135–39
  "immediatists," 6–7
  personal bravery of, 44
  rise of, 5–10
  unity of, 46
  weapons of, 45–46
Academy of Music, 2–3
"Accounts of the Pottawatomie Massacre"
    (Doyle and Wilkinson), 55–58
"Act to Punish Offenses against Slave
    Property, An" (Kansas Territorial
    Legislature), 48–50
Adair, Samuel, 15, 54
Adirondack Mountains, 11
African Americans. *See also* slave
    insurrections; slavery
  abolitionists, 5, 43–47
  adoption of, 7
  attitudes toward, 8, 9–10, 11
  Brown's criticism of, in "Sambo's
    Mistakes," 9–10, 11
  Brown's faith in, 29
  Brown's plan for Southern "free state"
    and, 21
  Brown's relationships with, 8, 10, 34*f*
  Civil War soldiers, 70
  free community, Canada, 65
  Fugitive Slave Law and, 11–12
  Harpers Ferry raid and, 72
  schools for, 7
  timidity of, 9–10
Allen, Ethan, 111
American Anti-slavery Society, 6
American Colonization Society, 5
anarchy, 125
Anderson, Jeremiah (Jerry), 38, 72, 73, 74,
    75, 89, 100

Anderson, Osborne P., 27, 38, 65, 70
  "Voice from Harpers Ferry, A," 70–76
Appeal in Four Articles (Walker), 5
Atchison, David Rice, 55
Avis, John, 90

Baltimore & Ohio Railroad, 23, 25
Banks, Russell, 37*n*41
"Battle Hymn of the Republic," 33, 143
Bible, 102–3, 115
Black Jack, Battle of, 19, 58, 84, 146
"bleeding Kansas," 14*f*, 18, 19, 105–6
Bobbett, Alfred, 28*f*
"bogus legislature," 16
Booth, John Wilkes, 31
border ruffians, 36*n*24, 48, 61, 112, 113,
    114
Brooks, Preston, 17
Brown, Dianthe (Lusk), 4, 7, 144
Brown, Ellen, 16
Brown, Frederick, 7, 15, 19, 48, 145
Brown, Jason, 15, 19, 48, 52, 54–55, 145
Brown, John
  as abolitionist martyr, viii, 30–31, 32–33,
    77, 88–89, 120–21, 122, 127–29
  abolitionists and, 3, 4, 5–10, 20, 32–33,
    65–66
  Adirondack Mountain land, 11
  appeal requests for, 122, 126–29
  beliefs of, 4
  burial of, 32
  business ventures, 7, 8, 10, 11, 12
  capture of, 25*f*, 27
  character of, 8, 110–13, 117, 118–19, 121,
    122
  charges against, 29–30
  cheerfulness expressed by, 90, 94, 97,
    99–100, 101
  children of, 5, 16, 144
  chronology, 144–47
  as commander of armed forces, 66, 79
  conviction of, 8, 30, 89, 147
  decision to go to Kansas, 16, 49
  early life of, 3–5

Brown, John (*cont.*)
eloquence of, 28, 30
execution of, vii, 2, 31–32, 34*f*, 38,
109–10, 122, 147
family, 4–5, 118
final messages, 2, 31, 35, 85, 86–87,
88–89, 103
Fugitive Slave Law and, 12, 44
funeral service request, 100
hagiography, 36*n*41
Harpers Ferry raid, vii, 1, 71–76
insanity plea rejected by, 29, 86, 127
interview of, 76–84
justification of actions by, 88–89
in Kansas, 17–19, 22, 51–55, 59–64,
111–14, 135
legacy of, 32–35, 36–37, 37*n*41
Lovejoy murder and, 8
marriages, 4–5
in New England, 19–20, 59
news coverage of, 27, 104–10, 114–16
Northerners and, 32–33, 147
opening remarks at trial, 85–86
other names used by, 135, 146
plan for liberation of slaves, 8–9, 19–23
Pottawatomie Massacre and, 18, 36*n*21,
36*n*41, 55–56, 58
press coverage of, 30–31
relationships with African Americans, 3,
8, 10, 34*f*, 100
religious beliefs, 7, 22, 30, 78–79, 80, 85,
86–87, 89–90, 93–94, 95–96, 101–3
reputation of, 18, 19, 21, 51, 58–59
rescue considered, 109–10
sanity of, 116, 118–19, 122, 126–27
sentencing of, 30, 90, 147
slave rescue by, 22
Southerners and, 32, 33, 85, 122
Sumner attack and, 17–18
surrender of, 1, 76
tannery work, 4, 5
as terrorist, 3
Thoreau's defense of, 110–11
trial of, viii, 2, 27–32, 85–87, 89, 114, 126,
147
truce attempt, Harpers Ferry, 25, 75
United States League of Gileadites and,
46
violence used by, 18
as warrior prophet, 3
writings of
"Excerpts from the Trial of John
Brown," 85–87
"Idea of Things in Kansas, An," 58–62
"Interview with Senator James Mason,
Representative Clement Vallandigham, and Others," 76–84
"John Brown's Parallels: Letter to the
Editor of the *New York Times*,"
62–64

"Letter to Wife and Children from
Kansas Territory," 51–55
"Provisional Constitution and
Ordinances for the People of the
United States," 65–69
"Sambo's Mistakes," 9–10, 11, 145
"Selected Prison Letters," 88–103
spelling and punctuation, viii–ix
"Words of Advice: Branch of the
United States League of Gileadites,"
12, 43–48
Brown, John (grandfather of John), 95
Brown, John (Scottish tenor), 142
Brown, John, Jr., 5, 16, 48, 49, 52, 141–42,
145
emigration to Kansas, 15
Brown, Mary Ann (Day), 5, 16, 19, 144
Brown's desire to see, 101
Brown's letters from Kansas, 51–55
Brown's letters from prison to, 88, 101–3
Brown's request that she remain home,
91
financial and emotional support of, 91, 92,
96, 98, 99, 100, 101
Brown, Oliver, 27*f*, 28, 38, 52, 54–55, 72, 89
Brown, Owen (father of John), 4, 6–7, 144
Brown, Owen (son of John), 15, 23, 27,
37*n*41, 38, 48, 65, 71, 145
Brown, Ruth Mills, 144
Brown, Salmon, 15, 17–18, 36*n*21, 48, 145
Brown, Sarah, 5
Brown, Watson, 28, 38, 55, 71, 75, 76, 89
Brown family
in Kansas, 15–19, 60–62, 92, 118, 135
in Lawrence, Kansas, 17, 52–54, 60, 133
Pottawatomie Massacre and, 18, 55–58
Brown's Station, 16, 17
Buchanan, James, 29, 62, 130, 146

California, 15*f*, 43
Campbell, John, 63
Canada
Chatham convention, 65, 70, 139, 146
free black community in, 65
Harpers Ferry raid and, 123, 125
Cato, Judge, 60
Charlestown (South Carolina) *Mercury*, 31,
104
Chatham, Ontario, convention, 65, 70, 139,
146
Child, L. Maria
Brown's letter to, 92–93
Chilton, Samuel, 127
"Civil Disobedience" (Thoreau), 110
Civil War
African American troops in, 70
chronology, 147
Harpers Ferry raid and, vii, 1, 2
"John Brown's Body" and, 33, 35, 142–43
predictions of, 125–26

Clark, Edward, 133
Colorado, 14*f*, 15, 43
Colpetzer, William, 63
Compromise of 1850, 11–12, 13, 14*f*, 15*f*, 43, 48
Congressional Howard Committee Report, 56
Cook, John E., 20, 38, 71, 72, 140
Copeland, John Anthony, 25, 38, 72, 74, 76, 140
Coppic, Barclay, 27, 38, 71, 73, 119, 140
Coppic, Edwin, 38, 76
Cromwell, Oliver, 112, 113
Currier and Ives, 34*f*
Cygnes, Marais de, 63

Dakotas, 13, 14*f*
Dana, Richard Henry, Jr., 10
Darley, Felix O. C., 28*f*
Davis, Jefferson, 130
Davis, Lucius, 126, 129
Day, Mary Ann, 5, 144
Declaration of Independence, 66
deism, 4
Delany, Martin R., 21, 65
Democratic newspapers, 118
District of Columbia, 43
Douglas, Stephen A., 13, 15
Douglass, Frederick, 3, 8–9, 22–23, 65, 145
Dow, Charles, 51, 52
Doyle, Drury, 56–57
Doyle, Henry, 56
Doyle, James, 55, 56–57
Doyle, John, 56
Doyle, Mahala, 56
Doyle, Mahala, and Louisa Jane Wilkinson
    "Accounts of the Pottawatomie
        Massacre," 55–58
Doyle, Polly Ann, 56
Doyle, William, 56–57
Dred Scott decision, 20–21, 146
Du Bois, W. E. B., 3, 37*n*41

Emerson, Ralph Waldo, 2, 33
"En route for Harpers Ferry" (Strother), 26*f*
Evening Journal, Albany, New York, 104
    "From the Philadelphia Press," 109–10
"Excerpts from the Trial of John Brown," 85–87

Faulkner, Charles, 39, 76
fire-eaters, 31, 32, 33
First Brigade of Kansas Volunteers, 17, 51
Forbes, Hugh, 20
Franklin, Benjamin, 9
Free Soil Party, 10, 57
"free state"
    in Kansas, 54, 62–63, 113–14, 133
    plan to establish in South, 20–21

Free State Hotel, Lawrence, Kansas, 17, 55
"From the Philadelphia Press" (*Evening Journal*, Albany, New York), 109–10
Fugitive Slave Law, 15*f*, 79, 118, 129–30, 145
    abolitionist response to, 11–12, 43
    Brown's resistance to, 12, 44, 79–80
    provisions of, 43–44
    Thoreau and, 110

Garnet, Henry Highland, 12
Garrison, William Lloyd, 5–6, 36*n*41, 144
Geary, John W., 61
Giddings, Joshua R., 80, 136, 137
Golden Rule, 79, 80, 85
Graham, Dr., 61
Green, Beriah, 6
Green, Shields, 23, 38, 72, 74, 76, 140

Hairgrove, Asa, 63
Hairgrove, William, 63
Hall, Amos, 63
Hanway, James, 18
Harpers Ferry
    map, 24*f*
    targets in, 23, 131
"Harpers Ferry Affair, The" (*New Hampshire Patriot*), 104–7
"Harpers Ferry Conspiracy, The" (*Petersburg* [Virginia] *Express*), 107–8
Harpers Ferry raid, 23–28
    African Americans and, 72
    armory capture, 23, 72
    arms, 82–83
    bridges, 23, 25, 71
    Brown's justification of, 88–89
    chronology, 144–47
    Civil War and, vii, 1, 2
    elected officials, 39
    engine house, 71
    executions, 38, 140
    fatalities, 1, 23, 25, 28, 74, 75, 77, 140
    federal investigation of, 129–42
    funding of, 20, 59, 77, 125, 129, 131–42
    "John Brown's Body" and, 142–43
    militia, 39
    news coverage of, 26*f*, 27, 85, 104–10, 114–16
    planning of, 22–23, 59, 114, 131–42, 146
    prisoners, 73
    purpose of, 1, 77, 78, 84, 86–87, 139–41
    raiding party, 23, 38, 114–15, 140, 141–42
    rifle factory capture, 72
    significance of, vii, 1–3, 35, 120
    state justification for executions, 122–29
    storage of weapons for, 134–35
    surrender, 83–84
    truce attempt, 25, 75
    U.S. Marines, 27–28, 39, 73–74, 140, 147

Harpers Ferry raid (*cont.*)
  weapons for, 129, 131–42
  witness account of, 70–76
Harper's Weekly, 26*f*
Harris, Edward, 101
Hazlett, Albert, 38, 75, 76, 140
Henrie, John, 75
Higginson, Thomas Wentworth, 20, 59
  Brown's letters to, 91, 96
Hovenden, Thomas, 34*f*
Howe, Julia Ward, 2, 33, 142–43
Howe, Samuel Gridley, 20, 59, 137
Hughes, Langston, 3
Humphrey, Luther, 95
Hurd, H. B., 133
Hyatt, Thaddeus, 141

"Idea of Things in Kansas, An" (Brown),
    58–62
"immediatists," 6–7
insanity plea, 29, 86
"Inside the Engine House" (Bobbett), 28*f*
"Interview with Senator James Mason,
    Representative Clement Vallandig-
    ham, and Others" (Brown), 76–84

Jackson, Thomas J. ("Stonewall"), 31
Jay, John, 98, 101
Jefferson, Thomas, 4
Jesus Christ, 88, 93, 96, 121
"John Brown's Body," 3, 33, 35
"John Brown's Body" (Patton), 142–43
"John Brown's Body" (Steffe), 142
"John Brown's Parallels: Letter to the
    Editor of the *New York Times*"
    (Brown), 62–64
Jones, John T., 61
Jones, Ottawa, 61, 62
Jones, Samuel, 51

Kagi, John H., 20, 25, 38, 65, 71, 72, 74, 135
Kansas-Nebraska Act, 12, 13, 15, 15*f*, 48,
    145
Kansas Territorial Legislature
  "Act to Punish Offenses against Slave
      Property, An," 48–50
Kansas Territory, viii, 14*f*
  antislavery constitution for, 16
  "bleeding Kansas," 14*f*, 18, 19, 105–6
  Brown family in, 15–19, 22, 49, 51–55,
      60–62, 92, 118, 135, 145
  Brown in, 17–19, 22, 51–55, 59–64,
      111–14, 135
  Brown's report on conditions in, 59–62
  deaths in, 19
  free staters, 54, 62–63, 113–14, 133
  immigration to, 15
  Kansas-Nebraska Act and, 12–13
  Missouri Compromise and, 13, 15
  news coverage of, 105–7
  proslavery Missourians in, 16, 48, 53–54

punishment for antislavery activities in,
    16, 48–50
  slavery code, 16, 48–50
  struggle over slavery in, 13–19, 48–49
  violence in, 17–19, 35*n*19, 55, 62–63,
      145
  weapons used in, 132–34, 138–39
Karsner, David, 37*n*41

Lane, James, 51
Lawrence, Kansas
  Brown family in, 17, 52–54, 60, 133
  sack of, 17, 35*n*19, 55, 145
Leary, Lewis Sheridan, 25, 38, 72
Lee, Robert E., 1, 27–28, 39, 76, 140,
    146–47
Leeman, William H., 20, 25, 27, 38
Leonides, 22
"Letter to Wife and Children from Kansas
    Territory" (Brown), 51–55
Liberator, The, 6, 7, 110, 115, 144
Liberty Guards, 17
Lincoln, Abraham, 13, 31, 34, 35
Louisiana Purchase, 12, 48, 145
Lovejoy, Elijah P., 7–8, 32–33, 144
Lusk, Dianthe, 4–5, 144

Malin, James G., 37*n*41
man-land crisis, 4
Mason, James, 39, 43, 76–79, 118, 129
"Mason Report, The" (U.S. Senate Select
    Committee on the Harpers Ferry
    Invasion), 129–42
Massachusetts Arms Company revolvers,
    83, 134
Massachusetts State Kansas Committee,
    132–34, 138, 139
Merriam, Francis Jackson, 27, 38, 71
"Message to the Virginia Legislature"
    (Wise), 122–29
Mexico, U.S. war with, 11, 43, 110
Missouri
  Brown's raiding party into, 62
  proslavery residents in Kansas, 16, 48,
      53–54
  slavery in, 13
Missouri Compromise, 13, 14*f*, 145, 146
Montana, 13, 14*f*
Moses, 88
Mott, Lucretia, 98
Mount Gilead, 45

National Association for the Advancement
    of Colored People (NAACP),
    36*n*41
National Kansas Aid Committee, 132, 133,
    139
Nebraska Territory, 13, 15, 48
  map, 14*f*
Newby, Dangerfield, 25, 38, 74
New England, 19–20, 59

New Hampshire Patriot, Concord, N.H., 32, 104
"Harpers Ferry Affair, The," 104–7
news coverage
of Harpers Ferry raid and trial, 85, 104–10, 114–16
of Kansas events, 105–7
New York Herald, 3, 81, 119
New York Tribune, 63
North
criticism of Brown in, 32
Southern anger toward, 107–8
sympathy for Brown in, 2, 30–31
"Northern and Southern Newspapers React to the Raid and Trial," 104–10
"Northern army," 55
North Star, 8, 9

Oates, Stephen, 37*n*41
Oberlin College, 7, 10, 70, 144
Oberlin rescuers, 79–80
Old Testament, ix, 3
"Oppressed People of United States" Chatham, Ontario, convention of, 146
Osawatomie, Battle of, 19, 36*n*24, 53, 59, 61, 84

Parker, Richard, 85, 88
Parker, Theodore, 20, 59
Parsons, J. S., 65
Patton, William W.
"John Brown's Body," 142–43
Paul, 88, 97, 109
Perkins, Simon, 8, 11, 145
Persian Wars, 22
Petersburg (Virginia) *Express*, 104
"Harpers Ferry Conspiracy, The," 107–8
Pierce, Franklin, 117*n*7
"Plea for Captain John Brown, A" (Thoreau), 110–21
Poor Richard, 9
"Popular Sovereignty," 15
"Porte Crayon," 26*f*
Potomac Bridge, 23
Potomac River, 25*f*
Pottawatomie Massacre
Brown and, 18, 36*n*21, 36*n*41, 55–56, 58, 146
Brown family and, 55–58
witness accounts of, 55–58
"Provisional Constitution and Ordinances for the People of the United States" (Brown), 20–21, 27, 65–69, 78, 79, 146
armed forces, 66, 79
arms, 69
captured or confiscated property, 67, 68
marriage and families, 68–69
membership qualifications, 66–67
neutrals, 67–68

oaths and affirmations, 69
overthrow of U.S. government and, 66, 69
safety or intelligence fund, 67
voluntaries, 67
Puritans, 112

Quakers, 90
Quarles, Benjamin, 37*n*41

racial attitudes, 8, 9–10, 11
Ram's Horn, 9, 145
Realf, Richard, 65
Redpath, James, 18–19, 34*f*, 36*n*41, 37*n*41, 141–42
Reed, B. L., 63
religious revivals, 4–5
Republican newspapers, 116
Republican party, 130
"Resistance to Civil Government" ("Civil Disobedience") (Thoreau), 110
revolver pistols, 83, 131, 132, 133–34, 138
Reynolds, David, 29, 37*n*41
Robertson, William, 63
Robinson, Charles, 51
Rogers, John, 95, 103
Ross, Patrick, 63
Ruffin, Edmund, 31
runaway slaves. *See also* Fugitive Slave Law; slavery
Brown's plan for Southern "free state" and, 21
Brown's support of, 7
Fugitive Slave Law and, 11–12
in Kansas Territory, 16
Russell, Mrs. Thomas, 31

"Sambo's Mistakes" (Brown), 9–10, 11, 145
Samson, 88, 94
Sanborn, Franklin, 20, 21, 36*n*41, 37*n*41, 59, 141–42
Second Great Awakening, 4–5, 6
"Secret Six," 20, 36*n*41, 59, 146
"Selected Prison Letters" (Brown), 88–103
Seward, William H., 2, 107
Shannon, Wilson, 51, 52–53
Sharpe's rifles, 83, 105–6, 131, 132, 134, 138
Shenandoah Bridge, 25
Shenandoah River, 25*f*, 72
Shepherd, Hayward, 23
Sherman, William, 55
slavecatchers, 12
slave insurrections
Brown's faith in, 29, 82
failure of, at Harpers Ferry, 1, 25, 131
fear of, vii
Fugitive Slave Law and, 12
Turner, Nat, and, 6, 144
warning of, at Harpers Ferry, 25
slavery. *See also* runaway slaves
calls for end to, 6–7, 116–17, 144
death of Brown and, 109–10

slavery (*cont.*)
  in Kansas Territory, 16
  sectional conflict over, 124–26, 129
  as sin, 4, 6
  Southern protection of, 123
  violent overthrow of, vii–viii, 3, 6–7, 18,
    31–32, 49, 62–63, 65–66, 88–89, 103,
    124–25
  voluntary delivery of slaves, 67
Smith, Gerrit, 10–11, 20, 59, 81, 106, 138,
    145
Smith, Isaac, 132, 146
Snyder, Asa, 63
South
  anger toward Brown, 31, 85, 107–8, 122
  anger toward the North, 32, 107–8
  Brown's plan to attack, 19–23, 65–66
  Civil War and, 2
  plan to establish "free state" in, 20–21
South Carolina, 2
Southern Rights Associations, 2
Stark, John, 111
Stearns, George, L., 20, 59, 133, 134, 136,
    137, 138
  Brown's letter to, 100
Stearns, George, L., Mrs., 96
Steffe, William, 142
Stevens, Aaron D. (A. D.), 20, 25, 38, 65, 71,
    72, 75, 140
Stilwell, Thomas, 63
Stowe, Harriet Beecher, 35
Strother, David, 26*f*
Stuart, J. E. B., 27, 39, 76
"Subterranean Passway," 9, 19–20
Sumner, Charles, 17–18, 55, 107, 145

Taliaferro, William B., 126
Tappan, Arthur, 6
Tappan, Lewis, 6
Taylor, Stewart, 38, 71
Texas, 43
Thermopylae, 22
Thirteenth Amendment, 147
Thompson, Adolphus, 72
Thompson, Dauphin, 38, 89
Thompson, Henry, 36*n*21, 52, 54–55, 61
  widow of, 91, 92
Thompson, William, 27, 38, 89
Thoreau, Henry David, 2, 33
  defense of Brown by, 110–11
  "Plea for Captain John Brown, A," 110–21
Tidd, Charles Plummer (C. P.), 20, 27, 38,
    65, 71, 72
Tilden, D. R.
  Brown's letter to, 99–100
Transcendentalists, 36*n*41, 110
transcontinental railroad, 13
Turner, Nat, 6, 144

Uncle Tom's Cabin (Stowe), 35
Underground Railroad, 70
"Union Meeting," Academy of Music, 2–3
United States League of Gileadites, 12,
    43–48, 145
  formation of, 46
  members, 46, 47–48
  officers, 46, 47, 82
  resolutions of, 46–47
U.S. Constitution
  armed insurrection and, 140–41
  Provisional Constitution and, 66
  Thirteenth Amendment, 147
U.S. Marines, 27–28, 39, 73–74, 140,
    146–47
U.S. militia, 140–41
U.S. Senate Select Committee on the
    Harpers Ferry Invasion
  "Mason Report, The," 129–42

Vaill, H. L., Brown's letter to, 93–94
Vallandigham, Clement, 39, 76, 78–82, 114,
    120
Villard, Oswald Garrison, 30, 36*n*41
Virginia Legislature, Wise's message to,
    122–29
"Voice from Harpers Ferry, A" (Anderson),
    70–76

Walker, David, 5, 6
Walker, William, 117
Washington, Lewis, 39, 73, 119
weapons
  ammunition, 131
  funding of, 20, 59, 77, 125, 129, 131–41
  Massachusetts Arms Company revolvers,
    83, 134
  revolver pistols, 83, 131, 132, 133–34, 138
  Sharpe's rifles, 83, 105–6, 128, 131, 132,
    134
Weld, Theodore Dwight, 6
westward movement, 4
Whittier, John Greenleaf, 34*f*
Wilkinson, Allen, 55, 56, 57–59
Wilkinson, Louisa Jane, 56
Wilkinson, Louisa Jane, and Mahala Doyle
  "Accounts of the Pottawatomie
    Massacre," 55–58
Wilson, Henry, 115
Wilson, Hill Peebles, 37*n*41
Wise, Henry, 29, 31, 39, 76, 104, 109–10, 119
  "Message to the Virginia Legislature,"
    122–29
  respect for Brown by, 122
"Words of Advice: Branch of the United
    States League of Gileadites"
    (Brown), 12, 43–48
Wright, Elizur, 6